Earning and Keeping Customer Loyalty Made Easy
by Roy Hedges
© 2000 Law Pack Publishing Limited

Reprinted 2001

10-16 Cole Street London SE1 4YH
www.lawpack.co.uk

LAWPACK

ISBN 1 902646 57 6

658.812

EARNING AND KEEPING CUSTOMER LOYALTY MADE EASY

LAWPACK

Table of contents

10047156
658.812

 # Introduction

Customer service began in Jamaica

The above statement is true as far as I am concerned, for it was in Jamaica I first realised the benefits a friendly welcome and a positive attitude could have to a business – your business. It seemed every person I came across in Jamaica was smiling; they were happy to be alive and the only thing they wanted to do was to satisfy my needs. The smiles and cheery banter were infectious. Before long, I was feeling on top of the world. In every store, shop, restaurant or market stall I visited, as soon as I made a request or posed a question, the response I received was instantaneous and sincere. The reaction never faltered – the same two words were used everywhere I went. On this trip I became aware that those two simple words must be the foundation of good customer relations. The two words I kept hearing? 'No problem', accompanied by the biggest smile I ever saw, each and every time they were uttered.

Deeply impressed, I began using these two words from the moment I returned to the office. My fellow workers thought I had been affected by the sun, but within a day or two the atmosphere at work began to change. From that moment on, the office became a much more pleasant place to be. Not only did work levels improve, but everyone became friendlier towards each other and started to work better as a team. Utilising customer service practices internally does provide a gratifying environment that will reflect on your external patrons. Use these two words every time you answer a customer's query and note the improvement in their loyalty.

Customer service affects all of us, every day, in our working and private lives. You do not have to be in direct contact with customers to influence the way they feel about the firm who employs you. Poor workmanship on the factory floor and late deliveries, noticed and remembered by customers, can have disastrous effects on your wages and job security in the long term. Your customers are important to you – without them your business couldn't survive. It takes a great deal of energy and money to establish a customer base, so it makes sense to look after your existing, loyal customers. Taking a selfish point of view, it is far more cost effective to retain customers than to keep replacing them with new ones.

Anger, frustration, and disappointment are the language of customer service. It is a language you must learn if you wish to compete in an increasingly aggressive market. This book teaches you the correct vocabulary to use, and spells out how to:

- turn disgruntled customers into satisfied ones;
- make satisfied customers loyal customers;
- deal with irate telephone calls and exert a calming influence;
- handle complaints speedily;
- increase sales and make sure you get paid on time;
- demonstrate your commitment to customers;

If you run a small business, or are an employee, a manager of a large department, or controller of a vast organisation, then this book has been especially written with you in mind. It doesn't matter what section of the firm you work in, or the type of business or organisation you are in, you will always have customers to deal with, in one form or another. Although government departments do not wish to admit it, they too have customers to care for – us tax payers.

To retain customer loyalty, and have them happily coming back year after year, is not the impossible task it may first appear. All it takes is a little common sense, mingled with your firm's existing business methods. By reading through the following chapters, you will be given a demonstration of how this can be achieved and all those questions you are yet to realise you needed to ask will be answered. 'No problem.'

Is customer loyalty essential?

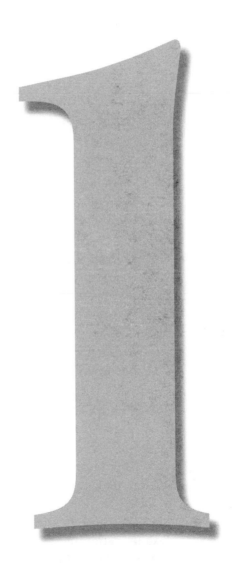

Chapter 1

Is customer loyalty essential?

What you'll find in this chapter:

⟹ Are customers always right?

⟹ Reasons customers get irritated

⟹ Why you lose customers

⟹ Why you should worry

⟹ What customers expect from you

⟹ The benefits of customer loyalty

⟹ Check your commitment to customer care

CAUTION

REMEMBER, YOU ARE IN BUSINESS TO SERVE CUSTOMERS, TO SUPPLY THEIR NEEDS – NOT TO SAY 'NO'.

When you start a business, the initial aim is to get people through the door. The next stage is to turn them into satisfied customers. Finally, to ensure the success of your business, you need to turn all your satisfied customers into loyal friends. However, there is no easy way to do this. It will take lots of time and hard work. Once you have achieved this aim, the next problem will be how to retain that loyalty.

Returning to the introductory question, we all know the answer has to be a resounding 'yes', if only from a selfish point of view. Putting customers first is what turns small unknown businesses into the household names of the future. To a lot of people, the above question must seem a stupid one. It is, but if you have ever been left hanging on the telephone or kept waiting to pay for your purchases at cash tills whilst assistants stand chatting to each other, you'll realise a lot of firms do not consider customer loyalty essential. You know how frustrating and annoying these situations can be, and your customers will feel exactly the same if they have to contend with indifferent members of your staff. So don't subject your hard-won customers to this type of situation. They deserve much better treatment – give it to them.

Unfortunately, customer service is one of those things nobody ever notices, unless it is very poor, then they'll observe and moan about the lack of it. Very rarely do satisfied customers praise a firm whose level of customer care is exemplary. Only a loyal customer will provide written compliments, rewarding you with letters of recommendation that can be used in your sales literature.

Patrons deserve and must be treated with respect. They should not be expected to put up with shoddy goods, or be served by belligerent staff. Interest in your customers' well-being affects everyone in your organisation, whatever its size. Gone are the days when nationalised industries could ride rough-shod over customer's feelings. These organisations have now joined the competitive world and their attitude towards customers has changed. Even these mighty companies have discovered that looking after one's customers and their needs is far cheaper than constantly searching for new clientele.

However, happy, satisfied customers are not your best advertisement. Rather, it is the loyal ones who serve you best, simply by telling their friends and acquaintances about your business and the excellent level of service you offer. These priceless free advertisements put more profits into the bank than any other form of promotion.

Therefore, if you intend staying in business for a very long time, the answer to the opening question must be 'yes'. Showing purchasers you really value their patronage will make them frequent buyers of your products or services. You will, however, have to earn your customers' loyalty, and it isn't something you can earn overnight. The process will be an extremely long one, but the end results will be worth the efforts made.

WHAT IS YOUR FIRM'S BIGGEST ASSET? IS IT PREMISES? STOCK? SALES LEDGER DEBT? AN EXCELLENT WORK FORCE? NO, IT IS NONE OF THESE THINGS. YOUR MOST VALUABLE ASSET IS A LOYAL CUSTOMER.

Are customers always right?

No matter how uncompromising a customer may be, if he or she is endlessly grumbling, it is you, not the customer, who is in the wrong. So yes! The customer must be right. Of course, there are exceptions to any rule, as you will see in chapter 5. In any misunderstanding you may have with a customer, you are going to find yourself in a no-win situation. Therefore, it is far better to prevent problems arising initially, than to try to talk your way out of them. So what can you do?

One advantage small businesses have over their larger rivals is flexibility. They can bend more easily to the special needs of customers and react more swiftly to a dispute. The most important aspcct of all is that the person at the top is on hand to reassure the customer. After all, it is he or she who has most to lose if the customer turns and walks away.

The first thing you must do when faced with an irate customer is pacify them, then if the dispute is about:

- damaged goods – change them instantly and without question;
- poor service – retrain your employees;
- misinterpretation of terms of trade – simplify them;
- misconstruing instructions – look for unsophisticated ways to use your products or rewrite your instruction manuals.

Invariably, you will be required to look inside your own organisation to discover the relevant grounds of any complaint. Removing the root cause will prevent uncomfortable situations from arising in the future. Chapter 4 will tell you how this can be achieved.

A paramount requisite in attaining this level of service is proper training. This training should not be restricted to customer service personnel or sales staff, but should include everyone employed in your business, irrespective of its size or their position.

For the small business, training needn't be an expensive exercise. This book, and in particular chapter 7, is designed to provide you with the knowledge required to undertake any training and to ensure, as far as customer relationships are concerned, that you stay one step ahead of your competitors at all times.

Reasons customers get irritated

There are some people, when confronted with a question or problem posed by a customer, who refuse to admit they do not know the answer. They believe that acknowledging a lack of information on a particular subject belittles them. So they tend to babble on about this and that and the customer becomes even more confused and bewildered than when they brought the matter up originally. You cannot be expected to know everything. Admitting this is not a sign of weakness, but shows strength of character that buyers or shoppers will respect. It is far better to simply say, 'I'm unsure how this gadget works, but I can find out for you if you don't mind waiting a few seconds', than to pretend you know something you don't. It's little weaknesses like these that inflame customers.

There was a time not too far distant when we in the British Isles tolerated poor service and shoddy products. Thankfully, that is now changing, but we still have a long way to go. Since the introduction of cheap air fair we travel more, especially to the United States of America, where first rate service has become an established part of everyday life. Now the standard reached over there is rapidly becoming the norm over here.

In addition to the items already listed, what infuriates me personally is:

- the 'I couldn't care less' attitude of staff;
- employees who simply go through the motions of assisting but in fact do little;
- people who are afraid to look you in the eye and who are unemotional.

Of course, there are other acts of non-service unrelated to raising complaints. Those associated with a dishonest salesperson, for example:

- blatant craftiness or unfairness;
- selling of unwanted goods or services;

- intentionally quoting unrealistic low estimates.

Then, on the physical side, there are other things that can give rise to customers' irritation. These include:

- late or non-delivery of goods ordered;
- wrong size or colour of items delivered;
- incorrect invoicing or pricing.

CIVILITY COSTS NOTHING, YET IT CAN DO MORE TO BOOST YOUR TURNOVER THAN A LOT OF EXPENSIVE ADVERTISING.

No firm should tolerate irate customers. Instead, business people need to be assured that their staff have been trained correctly, so staff will know how to react to all customers, whether they are complaining or not. Your customer care policy should also ensure training is not a one-off work-out, but a continuing, improving process.

It is not only the grumbling customer for whom you must go the extra distance, but also all those wishing to trade with you. Furthermore, polite service is not to be restricted to customers – it must run through every internal department. The reason for this last statement will become clear as you progress through this book.

Why you lose customers

All businesses lose customers for one reason or another. It's a fact of life that sometimes can't be helped. A majority of those people who purchase your wares will be satisfied if you simply give them what they want, when they want it. Others won't complain about poor service, late or non-delivery, or poorly manufactured products. They will simply shop elsewhere.

CUSTOMERS WHO ARE POORLY TREATED ONLY HELP ONE PERSON – YOUR COMPETITOR.

The cost to you of these lost customers cannot be measured at the price of a single sale, but as a whole lifetime of sales you are losing. Eventually, when your customers do get the service they want, you mustn't simply put your feet up, relax and forget about them. Customer service must be a continuous process. You must always be on the lookout for new methods to please your buyers. Keeping one step ahead of your customers' expectations is guaranteed to bring loyalty – and this is what really counts.

There will be times when the service you offer your customer exceeds their wildest dreams, but you will still lose them. Why is this? Customers can be lost due to reasons beyond your control, reasons you'll have to accept, such as their death, or their movement out of the area. Additionally, you will also lose customers because prices are cheaper elsewhere, and because your staff are lethargic and unconcerned about their needs. Unfortunately, there is absolutely nothing you can do to stop the first two situations from occurring. The third is purely a matter of economics, and only you will be able to decide if your prices can be lowered. However, you can do something positive to halt the drift of customers seeking alternative sources of supplies – re-train your employees.

The aim of every businessperson or manager must be to abolish rude, incompetent staff, particularly those employees who have an 'I only work here' type of attitude. From a customer's viewpoint, such staff appear to have no drive or desire to resolve their problems or assist them with their purchases.

One of the most common areas of customer frustration is the telephone. If, for example, someone has been stuck with a four-foot bed, instead of the five-foot one ordered, or they discover some alien creature in their corn flakes, normally their first reaction is to pick up the telephone and complain. Regrettably, that is not as easy as it sounds, especially if they get through to an automated answering system.

RESOLVING COMPLAINTS BEYOND A CUSTOMER'S EXPECTATIONS IS A MARKETING TOOL NO BUSINESS SHOULD BE WITHOUT.

When a customer initially dials your number they are calm and reasonable. After listening to a stream of recorded messages telling them to press this button or that, they begin to get a little edgy. It becomes another story, however, when they've being left waiting in an endless queue. Their tempers will have a tendency to get frayed around the edges in these situations. What they really want is a human being to whom they can air their grievances. Of course, once the customer is through to an actual member of staff, their frustrations explode, and an innocent person has to take the full blast of their abuse.

Keeping customers satisfied is at last being recognised as a way of competing in today's marketplace. Unfortunately, there are no set rules for dealing with complaints. The method used to pacify an angry customer by a firm manufacturing or selling low-cost items will vary enormously to one selling more costly priced goods or services.

For example, the former company can usually settle the matter by sending a letter of apology and enclosing a money-off voucher. The latter firm, on the other hand, will need to use a more diplomatic approach, preferably by someone with authority who can offer a more substantial form of compensation. This authority figure will need to take on the role of mentor, removing all doubt and fears the customer may have about their decision to purchase the item in question. Customers must be reassured that their decision to purchase the chosen item from you was the right one.

TURNING A SATISFIED CUSTOMER INTO LOYAL ONE REQUIRES SOMEBODY TO DO SOMETHING. THAT SOMEONE IS YOU. NO ONE ELSE CAN OR WILL DO.

Bringing smiles into your customer service, whether face-to-face or on the telephone, goes a long way to calming down irate customers. In later chapters you will be shown how to turn complaints into profitable repeat business. Some people have a natural talent for soothing annoyed customers, while other members of staff will need a few guidelines to achieve the same results. This book provides all employees with the right answers.

Remember, customer care doesn't just happen, you have to work at it and make it come about. Furthermore, customer care training shouldn't be restricted just to sales or customer service employees. It must include all employees, particularly those staff whom have regular contact with your customers, such as credit control personnel, service engineers or delivery people.

note

Sometimes, the reason you lose valuable customers is because the gap between the service you promised and its performance is too great. Customers will not hang around while you sort out your inadequacies. The most likely cause of customer care policies failing is:

- lack of commitment by managers and staff;
- insufficient training;
- reluctance to permit staff to use their initiative;
- failing to reward or motivate employees (see chapter 8).

When you inform customers of your intentions relating to the kind of service they can expect, make sure you don't go overboard and exaggerate. Do exactly what you say you'll do, perhaps more, but certainly not less.

Why you should worry

WORRYING ABOUT CUSTOMER SATISFACTION IS LESS STRESSFUL THAN WORRYING ABOUT A FAILING BUSINESS.

Providing your competitors with a steady stream of customers disgruntled by the level of service you offer is not a sound business move. So you do need to worry, if only for your own self-preservation. The impression may have been given so far in this book that customer care is all that matters in business. Whilst it is important to look after your customers, without a product or service people really need, all the customer care in the world will not make your business successful. Those goods also need to be:

- reliable and in demand;
- priced at a figure customers are prepared to pay;
- easily accessible.

At one time customer care was, and to some extent still is, an ideal tool for increasing the market share for your products. In today's marketplace, customer service becomes a protective requirement that is needed to safeguard your business. For example, if you provide customers with an additional service, such as home delivery, tomorrow your competitors will be offering the same service, and perhaps something a little extra.

Looking after your customer's interests should not be restricted to the time of purchase. After-sales attention in some service industries may be more important than an abundance of smiles and pleasantries at the time of purchase. Catering to a customer's interests after they have bought from you is covered in later chapters.

Never say, 'I don't have to worry about customer service', because you do, if you want to stay in business and remain competitive. This equally applies if you are in a monopoly position now, because it won't be like that forever. You only have to look at the electricity, gas and water companies to understand why customer service should never be neglected in any type of industry. When they were nationalised industries, customer care seemed to be bottom of their list of priorities. These days, they are pulling out all the stops to be one step ahead of their competitors. They have finally woken up to the importance of retaining customer loyalty, because now their survival is at stake.

If, on the other hand, you think because your goods or services are cheaper than your rivals, you don't have to bother offering your customers a service, think again. To a lot of potential customers, price is not always the deciding factor when making a substantial purchase such as home improvements or buying a car.

What customers expect from you

Customers want you to be fair and honest in your dealings with them. They would like to place their faith in you, and expect you to be consistent and truthful. Furthermore, they depend on receiving from you:

- friendly and courteous attention;
- reliability of products or service
- trust that their complaints will be dealt with promptly and fairly;
- deliveries will arrive when promised;
- all work to be carried out professionally and without fuss;
- the assurance that any rubbish will be cleared away.

The last item is in respect of trades people who are also required to leave premises neat and tidy.

CUSTOMERS DO NOT WISH TO KNOW ABOUT YOUR PROBLEMS. ALL THEY WANT TO KNOW IS THAT YOU CAN SUPPLY WHAT THEY WANT, WHEN THEY WANT IT – CHEERFULLY.

Fostering customer relationships alone isn't always sufficient. It is vital to go beyond customers' expectancies and provide that additional service. Never wait until your competitors have introduced new customer services. Always be the instigator. It is far better to be a leader than a follower.

For small businesses, it is a requisite that they build relationships based on customer confidence. The sensible use of customer information will play a pivotal role in achieving this aim. Because of the importance customer data plays in helping you stay one step ahead of the competition, chapter 6 has been devoted to this subject. The only way you can be certain of knowing what your customers expect from you is to listen to them. In later chapters we shall demonstrate how to get your customers to complain, and why it is important to you that they do.

Raising customer confidence in your business should be the aim of everyone working in your firm, whether they be employee or employer. How to carry out this level of service in operational terms is the object of the middle chapters.

The benefits of customer loyalty

Being aware of the many benefits good customer relationships can bring to your business is the first step in your firm's growth. The loyalty of your customers should therefore be as important to you as having the best products or services in the marketplace. When it comes to advertising, the quality of your customer service needs to become one of your key selling points, in addition to any other benefits your product may offer the purchaser.

Definition
CUSTOMER SERVICE CAN BE CONSIDERED **PROFICIENT** WHEN YOU PUT RIGHT WHAT HAS GONE WRONG. IT IS **EFFECTUAL** IF THE GOODS SUPPLIED DON'T NEED FIXING.

It was suggested earlier that cheaper prices could be one reason why customers go elsewhere for their purchases. However, price alone is not usually the sole cause of defection to a rival. If you dig deeper, you'll find customers routinely couple the price issue with one or more other motives, such as:

- repeated experiences of discourteous service;
- the belief that they're getting poor value for money;
- having become a victim of unreliable delivery.

The major benefits customer loyalty will bring to your business can be listed as follows:

- competitive advantage;
- higher profitability;
- allows you to ride seasonal lows;
- improve employee relations.

Over a period of time, the trust of loyal customers begins to extend from the original items purchased from you to new products or services you have introduced by listening to their needs. The gains in additional profits are also brought about because sooner or later operating costs are reduced, so you will be able to sell more with less advertising. Most important are the many new customers you can gain through referral by satisfied clientele.

By this point, it is hoped you have realised how essential it is to retain customer loyalty. Now it is time for us to move on, and together we shall begin to get your customer care policies into operation. To gauge your commitment to establish and maintain an ongoing customer care strategy, take the short test you'll find on the next page now.

Check your personal attitude to customer care

For each question place one tick against the answer of your choice

1. It's Monday morning and the first customer of the day approaches.
   Do you think:

   a) Why me?   ☐

   b) Here we go again, then sigh.   ☐

   c) Let's make somebody happy.   ☐

2. A customer has a complaint. Do you think it is:

   a) A pain in the neck.   ☐

   b) More trouble than it is worth.   ☐

   c) Not a problem but a golden opportunity.   ☐

3. When a customer approaches you with a problem, do you tell them:

   a) It's not my job.   ☐

   b) Fill out this form and send it to the complaints department.   ☐

   c) No problem. How can I help?   ☐

4. If a customer asks for something you don't stock, do you say:

   a) Sorry we don't stock that item.   ☐

   b) You'll have to contact the manufacturers.   ☐

   c) No problem. I'll see who stocks this locally.   ☐

5. When faced with something new, do you say:

   a) I can't do that.   ☐

   b) It seems all right but …   ☐

   c) No problem. I'll give it a try.   ☐

For all a) and b) answers ticked score nil. For every c) answer ticked score 5.
If you score less than 25 read this book carefully and retake the test at the end.

Customers are your best friends

Chapter 2

Customers are your best friends

What you'll find in this chapter:

➠ Getting customers to remain loyal

➠ Knowing where to start

➠ Getting your priorities right

➠ Taking the initiative

➠ Developing an image

➠ Taking one step at a time

➠ A personal view of good service

CUSTOMER SERVICE STARTS WITH A SIMPLE 'THANK YOU', EVERY TIME A CUSTOMER TELEPHONES OR VISITS YOUR PREMISES. IT'S AS EASY AND AS CHEAP AS THAT.

It is only natural that you would wish to cherish your customers and treat them with respect. Business is about building long-term friendships and partnerships with your customers, not making one quick sale. Establishing the type of relationship where it is habitual for your customers to come back time after time takes dedication and hard work. Moreover, customer care is not the sole domain of those people at the sharp end of business, like salespeople or customer service personnel. It affects everyone. Its principles should run through every spectrum of business, from senior management to the most junior employee.

Treating customers as you would your best friend also means using another little word with a big meaning – that word is welcome. Making your friends welcome and thanking them for their companionship comes naturally, doesn't it? It should be the same with your customers. The most powerful words or phrases you can say to your customers are:

'You're welcome!'
'No problem!'
'Thank you!'

Remember them, and do not use them sparingly.

ALWAYS LET THE CUSTOMER KNOW YOU ARE PREPARED TO MOVE HEAVEN AND EARTH TO RESOLVE THEIR DISPUTE, OR TO MEET THEIR NEEDS.

What you do and say can either bring in customers or turn them away. First impressions certainly do count. Using positive instead of negative words will set the tone for an amicable long-term business relationship, or a befitting solution to a customer's problem.

To show you care, and I mean really care, about your customers, ensure that a smart, cheerful individual always meets them. When answering their telephone calls, make sure a happy, smiling, comforting voice is there to greet them. Customer service is all about being happy, friendly, truthful and sincere, so use friendly words, friendly gestures, and friendly smiles. Always enthuse about a customer's purchases and sympathise with their problems. Be positive and confident in your dealings with buyers. This is what helps to create loyal customers, not just satisfied ones.

Getting customers to remain loyal

BUYING FROM YOU SHOULD BE AN EXPERIENCE THAT IS SO GOOD CUSTOMERS WILL WANT TO TELL EVERYONE THEY MEET ABOUT IT.

All things being equal, getting customers to remain loyal to your business, its products or services, is difficult indeed, but if you don't understand the definition of 'Customer Service' it is almost impossible. One doesn't need lengthy quotations from dictionaries to describe this phrase, however. In commerce, 'Customer Service' is generally understood to mean providing an additional help, civility, or after-sales attention beyond what a customer would normally expect to receive. Why would you want to supply this extra service? Plainly, it is to get customers to return to your business time and time again and purchase more goods or services from you.

Now that you know what customer service really means, and why we do it, you'll be able to commence putting together a workable and effective customer service operation within your business. Whatever method you choose to introduce a customer care programme, be sure to communicate this new service to your customers loud and clear. The care you are about to lavish on your clientele needs to outshine the service offered by your competitors.

This new system of care must have been deliberated upon, not hastily put together. Posting a simple statement on the firm's notice board, like the one shown below, just will not do.

> ## It's be nice to customers week
> ## — SO SMILE —

Going the extra distance for your customers should not be treated light-heartedly or seen as a one-off exercise. The introduction of any customer service or loyalty programme has to be meticulously thought out and needs to be a continuously improving policy. Whilst the decision to implement a customer loyalty programme can only be made by senior management or an owner of a business, once made, the resolve and input of all staff members must be incorporated, in order to implement this caring regime and its policy contents.

Knowing where to start

BETTER SERVICE SHOULD NOT BE RESTRICTED TO YOUR CUSTOMERS. IT MUST BEGIN WITHIN YOUR OWN BUSINESS, BETWEEN DEPARTMENTS.

So, now that you know the consequences of poor customer care, you must tackle the next big question, namely, 'how can we start to get it right and where do we begin?' It's already been established that the way to get a head start on superb customer care is to get your product or services right the first time. This immediately removes one area of discontent, and gives your customers one less cause to complain. It is also one way to ensure you get valuable repeat orders. Human nature being what it is, unless you have a very strong policy in place that is cleverly designed to stamp out repeat complaints, the slide back into the old 'couldn't care less attitude' is destined to occur. Having read this far, you hopefully now agree that the only place you can start your customer care programme is from within your own organisation.

Furthermore, this programme should begin from the top and work its way down through the business structure. Some business owners and managers quite wrongly think customer service is only for sales or customer service staff. Ideally, to ensure the success of your customer service programme and to avoid it being labelled shallow, proper time and resources should be allocated to getting your customer care policy up and running. Once this programme is operational, there needs to be a firm management commitment towards continuous training and improvement.

PROVIDING EMPLOYEES WITH THE CONFIDENCE TO ACT POSITIVELY WHEN FACED WITH AN AWKWARD CUSTOMER IS THE ESSENCE OF GOOD TRAINING.

Adequate training will ensure all managers and staff have a common focus, that is, putting the customer at the centre of everything they do. This will make the customer feel he or she is important, which is exactly how it should be. Giving all employees some level of autonomy must be a prerequisite of any training you undertake, because there will be times when they will need to make some on-the-spot decisions, in order to maintain customer loyalty.

There are, of course, many firms or individuals providing adequate training facilities – for a price. The object of this book, however, is to provide you the director, manager, or owner of a small business, with the knowledge needed to assume the mantle of trainer. Before embarking on any training schedule, take the time to decide what your ultimate aims should be. For instance, perhaps you wish to:
- concentrate more on your customers and the level of service you give them;
- recognise their needs and discover how you can best serve them;
- improve contact with customers by mail, e-mail, and telephone;
- discover what makes customers choose your products or services;
- turn complaints into profits.

Your initial aim may only be to introduce one or two of the above items, then gradually introduce others over a period of time. But perhaps you feel brave enough to tackle all of those suggested, and a few more that you have thought of yourself. Whichever way you decide is right for you, then that's the way to go.

To reach a constant state of excellence, your firm must be devoted entirely to furnishing the best level of customer care possible. Everyone throughout the length and breadth of your business should be focusing their full attention on the needs of customers. Once the basic ground rules have been put in place, all members of staff have to be made aware of how you conceive customer care developing. They will also need to know the importance you are placing on customer service and your level of commitment, together with the amount of training they will be given.

Gaining customer loyalty is not just a matter of spending large sums on training, it is also a matter of combining a little common sense with the knowledge gained from this and the following chapters. Whatever you do, you must make sure that your customer service procedure is known by every staff member, and that it is actually being extended to the customer. That means getting out and about, sampling the levels of service you offer for yourself, by speaking to both customer and the shop floor staff.

IT'S NOT ACCEPTABLE SIMPLY TO GIVE GOOD SERVICE, CUSTOMERS MUST BE AWARE THEY ARE GETTING IT!

Of course, you will need to appraise continually the degree of care given to your customers. You must also be looking incessantly at ways to improve on the level of customer service you provide. Not only must customer service start at the top, but it should also begin with an overview of the level of service extended between internal departments and staff. The necessity of this course of action will become evident as the following chapters unfold.

Getting your priorities right

Naturally, your first priority is to the purchaser of your goods or services. Remember, customers unhappy about the products or service on offer generally prefer to vote with their feet, rather than to write or use the telephone to complain. In other words, don't be surprised when they look elsewhere for alternative products!

So, when setting up or reorganising your customer loyalty agenda, the questions you must be honestly asking and answering are:

- Are our products or services reliable?
- Are our customers satisfied with the level of service proffered?
- Is our complaints system user friendly?
- Do we listen to what our customers are saying?

MAKE IT EASY FOR CUSTOMERS TO PURCHASE YOUR GOODS, BUT ALSO MAKE IT EASY FOR THEM TO RETURN THEM IF THINGS GO WRONG.

When putting together your customer service policy, at every stage you must first think - customer. Then you need to judge how your product or service meets his or her needs – not from your point of view, but from the customer's.

Sometimes a customer will complain about a product, even though it's not actually the product that is at fault. They have the habit of including all sorts of information in their feedback, even if these thoughts are not particularly relevant. For example, they'll mention:

- a product's packaging;
- the attitude of employees;
- the accuracy of invoices or instructions;
- how the telephone was answered.

Each one of the above items will be crucial in the eyes of a customer. Your handling of this feedback could mean the difference between a satisfied, loyal customer, and a customer who decides to go shopping elsewhere. In truth, obtaining feedback from customers is the only reliable method for you to learn how your customers think. The best way to conduct surveys and use questionnaires in order to analyse such vital information is dealt with in detail in chapters 6 and 8.

A good way to begin to implement your customer care service is through the use of a policy document, the ideal instrument for training purposes. In this document, you can set out exactly how you expect your staff to behave towards customers. However, you must be careful that your customer care programme isn't used as an excuse for not bothering. You must therefore stress how you anticipate the requirements set out in the policy document to be exceeded and not to be considered the norm.

Interact with everyone when setting up your programme, and get together with the people who work with you on a regular basis. Listen to what your employees have to say – after all, they listen to what your customers are constantly saying. Encourage your staff to interact with customers whenever possible. This exchange is vital for your survival.

Taking the initiative

By responding to your customers' needs, you will be provided with a steady stream of satisfied customers, but by being innovative and going beyond their expectations, you will breed loyalty. Start by putting yourself in the customer's shoes. The next time you go shopping, think about how you wish to be treated and reflect upon the experiences you have. For the moment, answer the following questions, then do the couple of simple exercises that have been set for you.

- Would you stand for poor service?
- Would you warm to rude and inept staff?
- Would you accept shoddy goods?
- Would you shop anywhere you did not feel welcome?

Do your buyers have to endure any of the above?

Now let's do some exercises. There are no scores and your list can be as long or short as you wish it to be.

FIRST EXERCISE

Make a list of the components you consider contribute to superior customer service. For example:
- helpful, but not overbearing staff
- assistants listened to what I had to say
- they responded to my needs

SECOND EXERCISE

Make a list of the elements you feel contribute to poor customer relationships. For example:
- nobody cared
- waiting a long time to be served
- the assistant kept making excuses

BUILDING AND SUSTAINING RAPPORT WITH CUSTOMERS IS THE ONE SURE WAY TO FIND OUT IF YOUR CUSTOMER SERVICE POLICY IS WORKING.

Do the above exercises immediately after you have been shopping with your spouse, girl or boyfriend. Get them to assist you with their reactions on the way they were treated, then repeat the above exercises in your own business or workplace. Ask your employees and co-workers to complete these same exercises and compare all the positive and negative attributes. On completion of the study, you should have an idea what will make a good customer care policy for your firm. It will be advisable to reiterate the research from time to time to ensure your customer service is not deteriorating. Get feedback from your clientele constantly, and ask them to comment about the level of service you offer. Solicit their requirements. See chapters 6 and 8 to discover how to get and use customer feedback to your advantage.

When dealing with customers, never use negative phrases, and forget trying to use lame excuses on your patrons. Your buyers want to hear the truth. They do not want to hear what you can't do or why you are unable to do it. They wish to hear what you can do and when you will do it. Yes, you. Whether face-to-face or talking on the telephone to a customer, no one else will do, there is only you. Customers 'will also need to be assured they can rely on you.

Words or phrases you should never use:

'I/we can't/don't do that.'
'I'm just doing my job.'
'Sorry, we are about to close.'
'It's not my fault.'
'It's not our policy.'
'It's nothing to do with me.'

Taking the initiative means taking responsibility and exceeding your customers' expectations. It also means not blaming others, but taking personal control of the situation. If a buyer is having difficulties expressing himself, do what you can to help him. If a customer has cause to make a complaint, make it easy for them to state their problem. Don't have the print on your documents so small customers have a hard time reading it, not everyone has perfect sight. Remove all obstacles that prevent a satisfied customer from becoming loyal to your business. The next time you are face-to-face with an angry customer, try pacifying them with this simple expression, 'You have a right to be angry.' This phrase is guaranteed to work every time, taking the steam out of any outraged customer. Once the customer is calmed, react immediately to their dispute. Agree a solution, take responsibility for sorting out the problem, and then do it.

Words and phrases you should use:

'You're welcome.'
'No problem.'
'Yes, we can.'
'I'll do that right away.'
'Of course I can help.'

Being original in customer service terms will be a full-time occupation. Once your creative ideas have been in operation for a while, they will become accepted practice. However, the process will have to be repeated constantly. Keeping one step ahead of your customers' needs is one thing. Keeping one step ahead of your rivals is essential – if you wish to remain competitive.

Developing an image

Outstanding service is not the sole factor in obtaining a customer's loyalty. Before a customer converges on your business, you will need the right goods or services to satisfy his or her needs. Once you have the right products, their packaging must be eye-catching and appealing. Most importantly, your business must establish an image so your firm is instantly recognisable by its products, its advertising, and its customer service. After all, in the beginning, Hoover was just a company who made vacuum cleaners. Now the word is part of our everyday language. Your promotional material, invoices, and in-house displays should look professional and universal. Well-designed packaging and a company logo will serve as building blocks in your efforts to create an unforgettable image.

When developing your image, listen to what your customers are telling you. The name you give the business can have a profound effect on them; a catchy, easy-to-pronounce name that isn't too difficult to spell will always be a good one. Wanting to name the business after the founder is not unusual, but if this name doesn't slip easily off your tongue, consider changing the spelling or its pronunciation. This kind of familiarity with your company name will bring direct results. Both business-to-business and casual customers will be encouraged to buy your goods, even when purchasing items they've never bought before, thanks to the solid image you've created.

Once you have decided on your image, it must be communicated to every potential customer. Use the firm's name at every opportunity. Advertise, distribute leaflets and sponsor a local sports team, but make sure they have your firm's name or its product printed on their shirts. Advertising can be expensive, so budget carefully. Use part of your advertising budget on existing customers to enable your marketing policy to be cost effective. Don't forget to use a web page to get your image across – some ISPs will give you a free web site.

ENDEAVOUR TO HAVE YOUR BRAND IMAGE IDENTIFIED WITH GOOD CUSTOMER SERVICE.

Write to trade magazines or newspapers about your business or products as often as possible, especially when you have something fresh to say, like the arrival of a new product or a special sale. They might print it, and it's all free advertising.

The regular appearance of your name or that of your business in the press can be difficult at times, because you will not be having sales or launching new products very often. So what else can you do? When you have nothing new to say, make a statement, any statement, as long as there is some connection to your firm and its products. The secret of getting your name in the press is to make any statement you issue as interesting as possible. The tract must be believable and not too far out to make it sound laughable. It does not matter if the subject matter is only your own opinion, as long as you deem it to be possible.

Petrol engines will be extinct by the year 2005

The director of Petrolless Engines Ltd predicts that with the rapid advancement of their new sonar power electric engine, petrol and diesel driven motor vehicles will go the way of the dinosaurs, within five to ten years.

The above news clipping may be 100 per cent inaccurate, but the director of this firm is optimistic enough to think it is true. Besides, who will remember it in five or six years' time? In the meantime, you will have achieved your aim by getting your firm's name before the buying public. That's what really matters. When published, quotes such as the one above give credence to the individual or business who wrote it. Without costing a penny, you have a valuable advertisement promoting your business.

Taking one step at a time

You cannot rush into customer service. It is not possible to simply say, 'our customer care policy starts tomorrow'. Any new or improved policy will take time to introduce and will require careful planning. Your early activities can affect the way customers perceive your care programme, so you need to start slowly. However, your initial efforts must be concentrated internally. By offering the same level of service to your colleagues as you do to your customers, you begin to make a pleasant place in which to work.

The support you offer each other across departmental boundaries can be reflected in the way customers see your organisation. With no infighting, the ambience of the workplace is more relaxed. Customers, sensing this pleasant atmosphere, will feel comfortable, and in turn will become friendlier towards your firm and staff. As we have seen, friendly customers will purchase more from you and will remain loyal longer. Additionally, with no internal bickering, customers' complaints can be resolved more speedily. This in turn will translate into more sales and greater profitability for your business. Building and maintaining rapport with your firm's internal customers, your co-workers, is therefore as important as feedback from external clientele.

With an improved working environment, employees will not be looking for greener grass, but will be content to remain in your employ. This will equate into better levels of external customer care and lead to higher customer satisfaction rates. Satisfied customers will become loyal customers, returning again and again, increasing the amount they buy from you. Loyal customers will also be more inclined to tell others about the excellent service they receive from you, and more customers coming your way will necessarily bring more profits your way. The case for introducing a well-thought-out customer service programme inside your organisation on a step by step basis has now been presented. Are you starting to see its benefits?

A personal view of good service

For over twenty years I have been a customer of Barclays Bank. I would say that makes me a loyal customer, wouldn't you? During this period, only once did I have cause to test their complaints procedure. Happily, the problem was sorted out before I left the local branch. That is the kind of service I like. Every time I telephone for financial information, the calls are answered promptly, politely, and in a friendly manner. My statement arrives every month on the dot, and if at any time I am unable to reconcile it, I usually find the error is mine.

I remain a devoted customer of Barclays not only because I have very little opportunity to test the bank's complaints programme, but also because every time I visit a branch office, the friendly cashiers acknowledge me by name. That makes me feel good. Now, I know they only take my name from the paying-in book I've just passed across the counter, but it makes such a lot of difference to hear, 'Good morning, Mr Hedges', rather than the bland, 'Good morning, Sir.'

So, give a little thought to the words you and your staff use when greeting customers. Even slightly personalised comments will make them warm to your business and employees. It is important to remember that customers buy the salesperson before they purchase your goods or service.

Proactive customer service:
retail sector

Chapter 3

Proactive customer service: retail sector

What you'll find in this chapter:

- Going that extra mile
- Fulfilling customer needs
- On-line shopping
- Remaining competitive
- Discount and loyalty cards
- A personal view of good service

Whilst the manner of care in which we treat customers should be uniform, irrespective of whether they are consumers or business-to-business clientele, there are certain aspects of customer service that relate more to the retail sector, and vice versa. For ease of reference, separate chapters have been introduced for each section. Nevertheless, there is a cross-over of ideas, so it might be a good idea for you to read both chapters, irrespective of the sector in which your business trades.

Proactive customer service can lead to greater contentment at work for you and your employees. To achieve personal satisfaction through such service, you must develop your self-confidence, which means:

- believing in yourself;

- believing in your company's products or service;
- believing in your firm.

Turning satisfied customers into loyal shoppers and establishing long-term relationships with them has to be fun. Work must be carried out in a happy frame of mind, and your place of business must be a pleasurable place to enter. If such a situation is created, the first name to come to a shopper's mind will be yours. Therefore, you must do your best to ensure that a shopping expedition to your firm becomes a positive experience, not a chore.

When it comes to achievable levels of customer care, there are four basic categories: 'all right', 'good', 'excellent', and 'unforgettable'. To fall into the category of 'unforgettable', you must take that extra step, care for your shoppers, and listen to what they have to say.

THE KEY TO RETAINING A CUSTOMER'S LOYALTY IS TO DEVELOP THE ABILITY TO THINK LIKE A SHOPPER, NOT A BUSINESSMAN OR WOMAN.

Going that extra mile

Generally speaking, a customer wants to shop in unsoiled and appealing surroundings. They also need to be met by courteous staff, to feel secure, to be free from any hassle, and to have freedom of choice. Added to these basic requirements should be consistency and reliability of both products and service. To go that extra mile, you can:

- learn to cope with unusual situations;
- be flexible, especially if a customer wants to buy part of a set;
- make sure your customer service procedures help the customer, not you alone;
- let the customer know that they do really matter.

Welcoming signs as a customer enters your shop and a positive attitude from all employees go a long way in encouraging customers to relax and enjoy their time in your premises.

Let's face it, we all suffer from 'buyer's phobia' at some time or another. To overcome this little problem, all you need is a helpful, caring assistant to confirm that the decision you have made is the right one for you. It is all part of going that extra mile.

What is buyers' phobia?

Say you need a new suit for a special occasion. After spending hours sifting through racks of different suits, you spot one you like. Trying the suit on, you find it fits like a glove. Then, out of the blue, uncertainty creeps into your mind. Is it the right colour? Does it make me look too fat? Can I really afford it? When you have these doubts you know you have been struck with buyers' phobia.

Achieving unforgettable customer service requires total commitment from your entire organisation and demands conviction that the needs of the customers drive your decisions. To enable you to go that extra distance for your customers, you should introduce performance and service benchmarks you expect to be constantly exceeded. For instance:

EVERYONE IN YOUR BUSINESS SHOULD BE COMMITTED AND TRAINED TO PROVIDE THE HIGHEST LEVEL OF CUSTOMER CARE POSSIBLE.

- checkout queues not to exceed three people;
- all telephone calls to be answered by the third ring;
- deliveries to be made within 30 minutes of order;
- monthly management accounts to be delivered within three days of month end;
- telephoning customers when your engineer or salesman will be more than five minutes late.

Quality customer service requires four key functions to be working simultaneously to ensure total customer satisfaction. These are:

Pre-emption   You have anticipated correctly the products or service the customer wants, their needs are exactly met.

Conformity   Your products are constantly dependable.

Continuity   The level of service remains steady or is improving over a period of time.

Satisfaction   The customer leave your premises feeling the experience was a good one.

Now you may be asking, 'How will it be possible to check if my firm compares favourably with the competition?' And, 'How does my customer service rate against a shopper's expectations?' You'll get some answers to these two questions in the next section and in chapter 8.

Fulfilling customers' needs

Your products or services may be acceptable to customers today, but what about tomorrow? The tastes and requirements your customers currently exhibit might change. A competitor may open around the corner. If your products do not evolve along with customers' expectations, or your service standards deteriorate, then you'll have a downward sales spiral. However, constant interaction with your customers can avoid this happening. In effect, this calls for constant interaction between:

USE A FREEPHONE HOTLINE TO ENCOURAGE CUSTOMERS TO AIR THEIR VIEWS ON THE SERVICE AND PRODUCTS THAT THEY WOULD LIKE TO OBTAIN FROM YOU.

- management and staff;
- customers and staff;
- management and customers.

The best information can be obtained from those employees on the front line. If these people are listening to what customers are telling them, they can inform and alert you to the customers' needs. You could also ask the customer directly, by having your senior management conduct person-to-person interviews, or by providing shoppers with questionnaires. Most importantly, find out what your customers think of you. The method is immaterial.

Customer service type surveys can be a useful market research tool. This aspect of surveys is covered in the last chapter. A purely customer service type survey designed to gauge the level of service received could look like the sample on the opposite page. Added to the questionnaire could be spaces for the customer's name, address and telephone number. If you do choose to include this information, do not forget to mention that the supply of personal details is strictly voluntary.

Once these surveys have been completed, analyse their contents. The results should indicate the area of customer service future training should target. Of course, the questions used in your customer service questionnaire can be more detailed - it all depends on the amount of information you need. A word of warning: over-long questionnaires can put people off, so the feedback you receive based on such a questionnaire may not provide you with a true picture of how shoppers view your business and products.

How did we serve you today?

Please insert either '1' (excellent); '2' (good); or '3' (poor) in the boxes alongside each question.

a. How was your greeting when you arrived? □

b. Were you made to feel like a valued customer? □

c. Did the assistant listen to your problem? □

d. Were explanations clear? □

e. Did we indicate how long the enquiry would take? □

f. Generally, how was the service you received? *(tick one box only)*:

- Less than expected □
- Better than expected □
- Average □

Please list any other comments on the reverse.
Thank you for completing this survey.

Sometimes customers will provide unsolicited feedback, by way of letters of praise or complaint. Do not ignore these valuable lessons your shoppers are giving you in this very meaningful form. Letters written by customers who actively take the time and trouble to sit down and compose their thoughts can be more valuable to you than endless surveys. Ignore these letters at your peril.

On-line shopping

E-commerce is here to stay. Like it or not, sooner or later you will have to embrace it, either as a customer or to expand your business. Since its inauguration, there have been on-line retailers, banks, and insurance firms happily trading away. While the effects on the travel industry seem to have made the biggest impact on our lives, on-line share dealing is another area that is quickly becoming popular. Whatever service you may need, or products you wish to buy, they are waiting for you on the World Wide Web.

Whatever your views about on-line shopping, it isn't going to disappear. So if you decide to put your business on-line, remember the customer and do not default on the service you deliver.

For some unknown reason, on-line customers lack the patience of High Street shoppers. Perhaps it is because they know that your competitor is only a click away, should they become too frustrated with your web site. So ensure your web pages are easily accessible and that they do not take too long to download. Furthermore, ease of access between your web pages is as important as the accessibility of your site. If displaying catalogues, or accepting on-line orders, make your pages customer friendly. Most importantly, organise a secured site so payment may be made via the web.

Some of the failings I have encountered when trying to buy, obtain a share dealing service, or open a banking account on-line have been:

- purchases were not delivered as promised;
- failure to respond to e-mail enquiries, or the replies took over three days;
- complaints were not dealt with satisfactorily or speedily;
- passwords issued by stockbrokers and banks were not recognised when I tried to log on;
- the screen kept freezing;
- site inaccessibility.

The above problems seem to stem mainly from Internet-only businesses, but things are slowly improving. Do make sure your web site is one shoppers can applaud and recommend to family and friends, not one that causes them to complain. When your business is on-line, and orders come flooding in, try not to be complacent with customer service. It does count, on-line as well as off-line.

Remaining competitive

Constantly striving for a competitive advantage can be costly and time-consuming. No sooner do you come out with one scheme than your rivals have copied it. The original edge you had earlier gained can be quickly lost - a vicious circle. If you cannot keep one step ahead of your customers and the competition, it is unlikely you will remain in business for long.

In order to discover how you can make the best use of these new advantages, you must invest a certain amount of time and money. Unfortunately, this carries a certain amount of risk, particularly if the resulting ideas prove to be unsatisfactory with customers. If no studies are made, these risks could be avoided, but then you could be left without any possible advantages over your competitors.

DON'T FORGET TO USE E-MAIL FOR CUSTOMER SERVICE SURVEYS AND SPECIAL OFFERS.

Perhaps one of your 'competitive edges' is that you can offer lower prices than your rivals. Low prices alone can leave you unprotected against new contenders, however, especially if you are unable to obtain bulk discounting facilities to bolster your profits. Another disadvantage of using cut-pricing as your sole strategy is that customers sometimes link cut-prices to poor services or low quality.

If you wish to improve continually the benefits to your customers, you'll be required to survey the following areas of your business:

- modes and frequency of deliveries;
- method of service promotion, i.e. e-mail, direct mail, customer surveys, mail order;
- sales processing and after-sales service;
- customer friendly complaints system;
- improvement of training techniques;
- packaging;
- reduction of queues at checkouts.

In fact, every aspect of your business needs to be closely inspected in order to find ways of improving the service you give customers.

Removing departmental barriers so employees know the work different departments undertake provides a total view of the company and will allow them to deal with questions that would otherwise require the customer to be transferred to someone else. Providing customers with uniformity when they have a dispute is one method to secure their loyalty. Operating in this manner removes a customer's frustration and enables your staff to resolve the majority of a customer's problems on the spot.

Retaining the competitive edge can only be led by example, from the top. So, you up there, don't be secretive. Always involve your employees in your surveys. This will ensure their full co-operation and will make for good management practice. Finally, once you have decided upon a positive new strategy, tell everyone about it.

IF YOUR BOSS CAN MEET DEADLINES, DEAL WITH MUNDANE TASKS CHEER-FULLY, AND LISTEN TO CUSTOMER'S COMPLAINTS SYMPATHETICALLY, THEN SO CAN YOU.

Discount and loyalty cards

In order to encourage customers not shop at their rivals' stores, some of the larger retail chains and supermarkets have introduced loyalty and discount cards. Alas, whilst the first retail group to offer customers this incentive gained a marketing advantage, the playing field quickly levelled out when competitors jumped on the bandwagon. Now these retail groups aim to woo customers with add-ons such as discount fares and double-point promotions.

The idea behind the scheme is simple. The company in question implements the scheme by issuing every customer who applies, a plastic card. These cards record the number of points awarded or spent. Every time a customer makes a purchase in one of the group's stores, they are awarded a certain number of points for each pound spent. Customers can either have money-off vouchers to spend on their next visit to the store, or they can choose a gift from a catalogue or shelf. Each company has their own rules for converting points into cash or goods. Sometimes, however, stores do place restrictions on certain goods, such as pharmaceuticals.

From time to time, these retail groups provide further encouragement by using these loyalty cards as promotion material, making offers of double or treble points, instead of reducing prices. They are operating

WITHOUT A LITTLE OLD-
FASHIONED CUSTOMER
SERVICE, DISCOUNT
CARDS ON THEIR OWN
DO LITTLE TO
ENCOURAGE LOYALTY.

under the belief that when customers start to see their points accumulating, an in-built urge will make them return to that group in order to spend more, so their points total will grow even more quickly. However, discount cards can be self-defeating, because some shoppers hold cards for all stores. As the discount only amounts to a 1 per cent reduction of prices in supermarkets, the urge to remain loyal can soon evaporate, especially if a local store begins to offer bigger money-off reductions on their own products.

If you are a small shopkeeper thinking that you cannot compete with your larger rivals and their loyalty cards, think again. Whilst it may not be cost-effective to issue plastic cards to every customer, there is nothing to stop you having a few **'Thanks for your custom'** coupons printed. With a small computer you can even run these coupons off yourself. Try offering customers a free newspaper the next time they shop (if you are a newsagent), or a cash discount if they spend more than a specified sum the next time they visit your shop. These are only a couple things you can use to compete. With a little imagination, I'm sure that you could come up with something much better to vie with the big boys.

A personal view of good service

One of the best loyalty card schemes I have come across is the 'Advantage Card' from Boots the Chemists. In all of Boots' larger stores 'Advantage Points' machines can be found. You insert your little plastic card into the electric kiosk and details of special promotions instantly appear on screen. By touching the monitor where indicated, a voucher is released. Shoppers then take this to the cash desk and immediately exchange it for the current offer. Sometimes these vouchers are for money off, others offer a free product, and at other times customers receive extra loyalty points.

What I personally like about the 'Advantage Card' is Boots' generosity. It is not the fact they give four points for every pound spent. Supermarkets generally only give you one per pound. However, we must remember that the gross margins for the two groups may differ. When you spend £9.96 in a supermarket, points are awarded only on the £9.00. At a Boots store, advantage points are calculated as if the customer had spent the full £10.00. It can be very frustrating when you miss out on something extra for the sake of 4p, can't it?

Another aspect I like about the Boots loyalty scheme is the fact they haven't forgotten about customer service. On a recent visit to a Boots store, my wife and I spotted an item we had been seeking for some time. In our excitement we grabbed the item, which cost £30.00, took it to nearby till, and paid for it. We had really come to purchase a set of kitchen scales, so with the points earned on this additional purchase and those we had accumulated prior to this visit, we acquired a new set of scales using our advantage card. We were delighted with our purchases.

On our way out, we remembered two other badly needed items – make-up for my wife, and hair tonic for myself. Splitting up to get the separate items, we lost sight of each other. As a male shopper, I got a little agitated because I wanted to pay for my hair tonic and go, but my wife had our advantage card. The trouble was, it was double points day. Getting fed up, I made the purchase without the card and went searching for my wife.

When we finally caught up with each other, she was about to pay for her purchases. Explaining to the cashier that I had made a purchase a few minutes earlier without using our Advantage Card, the cashier smilingly suggested she could add the missing points to my wife's bill. During the course of the transaction, we mentioned our other larger purchase, to which the cashier replied: 'Did you get your free CD?'

'What free disc?', we asked.
'If you spend more than twenty-five pounds you can choose a free CD. The offer is displayed at the Advantage Point.'
'What's that?', we responded in amazement.

At this point, the cashier called over another assistant to tell us about the Advantage Points machines and the offers that they display. Then the helpful assistant offered to take back our original purchase, credit my visa card and re-sell the object to us with the free CD. We were doubly delighted. This story perfectly illustrates what customer service is really about. Boots clearly and demonstrably believe in going that little bit further to turn a satisfied shopper into a loyal customer.

Dealing with customers' grievances

Chapter 4

Dealing with customers' grievances

What you'll find in this chapter:

> ▶ Encouraging customers to complain
>
> ▶ Setting up a complaints system
>
> ▶ Monitoring customer problems
>
> ▶ How you can benefit from complaining customers
>
> ▶ A personal experience

One of the most annoying things, from a customer's point of view, is a company's failure to deal speedily with their complaints. To avoid falling into this trap, it is in your own best interest to settle disputes amicably and instantly. As far as the customer is concerned, tomorrow is too late. Of course, there will be times when the complexity of a problem requires an extra day or two to sort it out. Be that as it may, providing you keep the customer aware of what you are doing, time should not be a major issue.

Unfortunately, it is a recognised fact of life that disgruntled customers will broadcast their woes more regularly and more persistently than satisfied customers will shout about the good service and products they've received. Therefore, it is essential that you make your customer service programme your number one priority, which includes putting customer complaints at the top of your care list.

Here's another undisputed fact: only a small proportion of your customers will take the trouble to complain. If they have a grievance about the level of service shown to them, they would almost always prefer to shop elsewhere than to grumble. So it is up to you as an employee, manager, or small businessperson to encourage customers to complain. In fact, you should try and make it easy for them to complain. It is only through customers bringing to your attention defective goods or poor levels of service that you will be able to rectify employee's attitudes towards them. Only by listening to people's complaints and analysing their problems will you be able to develop new products or services.

The next time you are approached by an angry customer with a complaint, try handling them in the following manner. First of all, empathise with them. Tell them you know how they feel. Next, find out the type of assistance they need by asking questions and listening to their response. No matter what they say, agree with them and confirm they have a right to complain. Now, personally take responsibility for resolving their problem. Let them know your name, so they can follow up their query confident in the knowledge they know with whom they will be dealing. Give them an idea as to how you will go about handling their problem, or how long it will take before you can offer a solution. In no time at all, you will have a calm, satisfied customer, and they a friend they can rely on. Everyone will be happy.

YOU WILL NEVER GET FIRED FOR TAKING THE INITIATIVE IF YOU THEREBY MANAGE TO TURN AN IRATE CUSTOMER INTO A LOYAL, SATISFIED ONE.

LOOK UPON CUSTOMER COMPLAINTS AS OPPORTUNITIES IN DISGUISE.

Encouraging customers to complain

Too many businesspeople today feel swamped by complaints, so why should you be urging others to grumble? Believe it or not, a customer who grumbles can be your best friend. If handled correctly, such complaints can highlight problem areas within your business. Often you will find the best ideas stem from a complaining customer. A shrewd businessperson uses data gleaned from customers to improve products and service.

People who complain could be amongst your most loyal customers, especially when they perceive that their dispute will be taken seriously. But how do you urge customers to complain? One way is to advertise your complaint procedures in a brochure and include a form for customers to use if they wish. Have these tracts displayed around your store, or in places most frequently visited by customers if you are not a retail business. Draw their attention to how you welcome customers' criticism at cash desks or at the entrance to your premises. Place them anywhere a customer is likely to notice them.

You may also wish to include this information in sales literature, on till receipts, on invoices or despatch notes, and in advertisements. As some clients prefer to raise a dispute on the telephone, include a freephone number in your brochure to make it convenient for them to contact you. Whatever you do, never forget to acknowledge the complaint. Always inform the customer of what you will do to resolve the problem and how long you expect this action to take.

More positive steps you can take to encourage customers to complain are to:

- telephone customers haphazardly and ask for their viewpoints;
- ask customers how you can put things right;
- offer inducements to complete questionnaires;
- ask your employees.

In all circumstances, always acknowledge the customer's complaint in writing, unless of course the matter was actually resolved on the spot. A short letter, which thanks them for bringing the problem to your attention, will confirm you care. For instance, look at the example on the following page.

Dear Mr. Moanalot

Thank you for informing me of the problems you faced when visiting our store recently. These are currently being looked into. I expect to come back to you with a satisfactory solution within four days from today.

Should you wish to make any further enquiries into this matter, please contact me, my name is Roger. It would assist me if you would quote Ref: CP/789 in your correspondence. If you prefer to telephone, my extension is 123.

Yours sincerely

A simple note like this one is enough to tell your customers you take their complaints and comments seriously. Customers will be happily surprised by the effort you take to confirm that their problem will be resolved by a certain date. Combine such action with the other types of customer service previously described and you will be turning every one of your satisfied customers into loyal patrons.

Setting up a complaints system

Nothing hinders customer relationships more than unsettled complaints. In turn this can lead to a reduction in sales and affect cash flow. Having an easy-to-use system for handling customers' disputes will do six things for your business.

1. Allows monitoring of all complaints received.
2. Informs you which complaints are unresolved – and why.
3. Provides an indication of customers' requirements.

4. Permits you to modify existing products or develop new ones.
5. Keeps you one step ahead of competitors and customer expectations.
6. Helps you to reduce the number of future complaints by enabling analysis.

The first thing you'll need to initiate your new complaints system is a complaints form. Previously, we mentioned a brochure designed to make it easy for retail customers to raise a dispute with you. The following are some examples of the kind of information you'll need to take from this brochure:

- customers' name and address, e-mail address and telephone number;
- the type of complaint being made, i.e. returned goods, late delivery, poor service;
- a short description of the complaint;
- suggestions for general improvement to your store and service;
- what the customer expects you to do for them.

Devising a form that makes use of these criteria should be relatively simple. Just remember to make the completed document attractive, user-friendly and practical!

One such example is provided on the following page. The presence of account details on the customer complaints form conveys to the member of staff responsible for resolving the problem, the amount of cash the dispute is holding up. It stresses the urgency of the dispute and the need to come up with fast and amicable settlement.

IT DOESN'T MATTER WHO MAINTAINS YOUR COMPLAINTS RECORD – CUSTOMER SERVICE, CREDIT CONTROL OR ORDER PROCESSING STAFF – JUST AS LONG AS IT IS ACCURATELY KEPT.

As soon as any member of staff receives a complaint, he or she should complete a form similar to the one on the next page and send it to the department responsible for resolving the problem, i.e. if the dispute was in respect of short delivery, the form would be sent to the dispatch department. At the same time, a letter of confirmation must be posted to your customer, which confirms two things: the dispute is being resolved and the length of time you expect it will take. All incoming complaints must be recorded with the receipt date and dispute details in brief. When resolved, the complaint must be logged out, to confirm the matter has been satisfactory concluded.

Customer complaints form

Customer name: Account No:

Invoice total: Account total:

Complaint number and reference:

To: (internal department)   Invoice/Order Nos:

From: Date:

Dispute details/type:

Actions required:

Copy documents attached: Yes/no

To the above form a tear-off reply section should be added, for example:

Reply:

Further details required:

Completed by: Date:

Your complaint procedures can be implemented more thoroughly if they are included within your customer service policy document. In this document you will be able to emphasise the importance you place on all complaints being resolved within a pre-specified time schedule, for instance, within five to seven working days. Such a time frame is encouraged because the longer a dispute remains outstanding, the harder it is to reach a congenial result. People's memories fade and actual events become harder and harder to recall. If too much time elapses, you might find that the staff member who dealt with the query originally has moved on. The record log will enable you to monitor the situation and see that your wishes are being carried out.

COMPLAINTS CAN BE TIME CONSUMING AND COSTLY. TAKE THE TIME TO LOOK INTO WHY THEY OCCUR SO YOU CAN STOP THE SAME DISPUTES FROM RECURRING.

Monitoring customers' problems

In the retail world, most complaints will relate to damaged or unusable products, and late or non-delivery of goods purchased. Other disputes might arise through lack of service, such as unmanned cash points, employees ignoring customers' requests or the downright rudeness of staff members. With unserviceable goods you either replace them instantly or offer a full refund. As far as the shopper is concerned, the problem is solved. You, on the other hand, must now return the item to your supplier, who in turn will either credit the cost to your account or replace it.

By recording every grievance a customer brings to your attention, any problem area in your store will be brought to your attention. Here are a few things you could address when difficulties come to light:

- **Uncivil employees**; introduce group workshops and retrain those employees in customer service methods.

- **Poor telephone response**; train customer care personnel in modern telephone techniques, which should include methods to calm irate customers.

- **Late deliveries**; review your transport department operations, or if using an outside contractor, change the delivery firm.

- **Unusable products**; too many items needing replacing from one

EMPOWER EMPLOYEES TO MAKE ON THE SPOT DECISIONS TO PREVENT SMALL DISPUTES FROM TURNING INTO SUBSTANTIAL ISSUES.

source indicates poor quality control in the suppliers' production department, so either stop stocking the offending article or change suppliers.

In the business-to-business sector, the issue becomes a little more complex, largely because most sales are conducted on a 30-day credit cycle. If an irate customer believes his problems are not being addressed, payment can be delayed for anything up to two or three months. If too many customers are complaining and withholding payment, the repercussion on a small business can be serious indeed. Most frustratingly, sometimes the amount remaining unpaid does not even relate to the small sums in dispute.

If your business deals with exports, contracts can be involved, and the added complication of distances and foreign languages can bring you even more problems when an overseas customer has a complaint. In this area of business, transactions that monitor your customers' accounts and complaints really do become important.

Benefit from complaining customers

Turning complaints into profit is not too difficult, providing you keep accurate records and monitor them on a regular basis. Introducing an analysis of customer disputes on a monthly basis, perhaps alongside your other management reports, is ideal. In order to speed up the process of analysis, I experimented and found that classifying disputes saved a lot of mundane work. Numbering each genre of complaint turned out to be one of the better systems for this job. For example:

MONITORING COMPLAINTS IS A SERIOUS BUSINESS, NOT SOMETHING CREATED TO FILL THE HOURS BETWEEN NINE TO FIVE.

- accounts query   1
- goods returned   2
- late service call   8
- pricing error   12, and so forth

These periodic reports will supply you with much valuable information, and will give you details of the number of complaints received in a given month. Taken together, you'll have an instant picture of the problems your customers are encountering. Additionally, a report on the status of each query will tell you if your complaints system is working, or if employees are just paying lip service to your requirements.

Now, you may be asking, 'How will resolving disputes quickly benefit my business?' First of all, it builds strong customer relations. A decisive, swift approach to a problem will clearly show that your customer's trade is important. In time, they'll know that all problems will be dealt with immediately and without fuss. This knowledge gives your customers greater confidence in your products/services and your business. Therefore, they will:

- order more goods from you;
- recommend you to their friends;
- pay promptly;
- relationships between the two firms will improve;
- your employees get less hassle.

Sometimes a problem can be a little more complicated than you first thought, so it will take longer to resolve than the specified time suggests. Any complaints that fall into this category need to be chased up. When discussing the situation with the department concerned, point out the difficulties your firm may face if they don't get on with solving the problem. Next, give your customer a call to apologise for the delay. The consistent use of this technique is imperative if you wish to continue doing business with such customers.

A personal experience

Some years back, I was called in to help a business whose customers were not paying their accounts on time. After only a short spell, many had stopped trading with this firm.

From my initial survey of my client's procedures, there appeared to be no special reason for their customers' non-payment. The quality of work this service industry carried out was high, and the company delivered what it promised; yet customers still drifted away.

The credit control staff were friendly and treated their customers with respect. Dutifully they telephoned customers for payment on a regular basis, and they listened carefully to what the customer said. As they empathised with each customer, notes were taken about the customer's complaints, but yet again no money arrived. Upon further investigation, I noted that all the non-paying customers had at some time previously raised a complaint or two. It began to dawn on me that no one was doing anything to ensure these complaints were being resolved. Watching closely, I also noticed every time a controller received a complaint, they walked over to an unused desk in a corner of the office.

Opening the tightly packed drawers of this desk, I discovered nearly 2,000 unresolved complaints. No wonder customers had stopped paying! When I questioned the staff about their actions, they said that no one had ever told them what to do with the complaints they received, and whenever they approached their manager on this subject, he always stated he did not wish to be bothered with such trivialities.

After installing a complaints system, this firm's cash flow began to improve and their customers ceased to desert them. Most of the older disputes had to be written off because staff had left and nobody knew if the problem was genuine or not. It took some time to turn the situation around, but we did it in the end. Happily, the firm is still trading.

There is a moral to this story. Brushing customers' complaints under the carpet and hoping they'll simply go away is not a sound way to conduct your business. If this practice doesn't stop, your customers, not their complaints, are the ones most likely to disappear.

Hopefully, you now believe that resolving complaints as quickly as humanly possible is in the best interests for you and your customers. In resolving any dispute, try and present the customer with alternative solutions. For example, if a replacement article would take too long to arrive, see if another model would be acceptable.

Loyal customers will work for you: business-to-business sector

Chapter 5

Loyal customers will work for you: business-to-business sector

---

What you'll find in this chapter:

▐▶ Getting to know your customers

▐▶ Better sales performance

▐▶ Improving cash flow

▐▶ Product development

Taking that extra step towards better customer service when trading with other businesses should be a little easier to achieve. For one thing, encouraging your business customers to complain is not usually a problem. If your products are being used as part of your buyer's own manufacturing process, they'll not waste any time in informing you of complications. If the wrong size part is received or if the delivery is short, they will soon be screaming down the telephone at you, because your defective product can upset relationships with their customers. If this situation happens repeatedly, your customers will soon be seeking a more reliable supplier.

Customer service must be practised at every point of contact with your customer. Your sales representatives do it all the time, so why not your credit controllers, delivery personnel and anyone else who is in regular touch with buyers? Politeness, smiles, eye contact and a cheerful

INTERACTING WITH BUYERS IS ONE OF THE BEST MARKETING TOOLS AT YOUR DISPOSAL. USE IT CONFIDENTLY AND REGULARLY.

response when talking to or meeting a customer will do more for your business than all the discounts and cheap freebies imaginable.

IT'S A PITY LOYAL CUSTOMERS CAN'T BE INCLUDED ON YOUR BALANCE SHEET, AS THEY'RE SUCH AN IMPORTANT ASSET TO YOUR BUSINESS.

Getting to know your customers

Learning a customer's name and address is only the first step in getting to know them. If you want to ensure your service goes beyond your customers' anticipations, you must know as much about their business as you do your own. Examples of vital pieces of information your armoury needs to contain are:

- the type of business sector they trade in;
- what their current and future requirements are;
- who signs their cheques;
- who approves invoices;
- who checks your goods into their warehouse;
- who does their buying.

What really sells your business is its people. Businesses are people. So in order to build bonds between business personnel, you should encourage staff members who are in touch with your customers to meet up with their counterparts. Inviting them to your factory or the warehouse helps to develop rapport. Once you get to know your customers better and understand their needs, keeping in touch will be easier. The benefits of this last remark will become obvious when you read chapter 8. A relationship built on such knowledge will save time when a dispute arises and a speedy resolution is imperative. Find out how well you know your customers, or indeed the opposite member of staff with whom you are constantly in touch, by trying the short test that follows.

THIRD EXERCISE

1. Make a list of your ten biggest customers.
2. Itemise what each company and each department in that company does.
3. Name the manager and supervisor of each department and their extensions.

For example:
- Finance director
- Credit manager
- Warehouse manager

- Bought ledger manager
- Chief Buyer

Should you find yourself having difficulty in completing the exercise, pick up telephone, or better still, start visiting your customers to find the right answers. Begin in your own sales department – they should know what makes your customers tick. There are no rewards for getting this exercise right, but the outcome can be disastrous if you get it wrong. When you know everything you need to know about your ten biggest customers, repeat the exercise with the next ten, and the next, until you know all your customers intimately.

Better sales performance

Selling is learning what people want and then helping them to get it. I haven't written anything outstanding in that last sentence. It is the first basic lesson taught in any sales training seminar. Improving the sales performance in your business can be achieved by utilising the advantages of customer service.

ALWAYS MAKE CUSTOMERS FEEL VALUED. THINK OF THE ONE YOU ARE CURRENTLY TALKING TO AS THE MOST IMPORTANT CUSTOMER YOU HAVE.

Extending high quality and consistent customer service should become second nature to you and your staff. Once you can reliably demonstrate such service, new customers will be encouraged to purchase from you, and they in turn will introduce even more people, thus providing you with an upward spiralling sales pattern. Talking and listening to your customers provides the ammunition you need to help them. Businessmen and women do things or buy your goods not for your sake, but for their own, so when serving them remember to address their needs appropriately.

Surveying customers, whether for marketing or customer service purposes, is as significant a requirement in the manufacturing and service sectors as it is in retailing. The results of these surveys could become a powerful selling tool, since an awareness of the requirements of the end user can only help you increase sales. In addition to the summary of the consumer questionnaires, feedback from your actual buyers will lead you to improve your sales potential.

Unfortunately, there will still be times when people refuse to buy from you, in spite of everything you've done to discover what they want. Whilst you have discovered their basic needs, the customer may also have an underlying requirement he or she wants to fulfil, not previously made known to you. It is in your interest to be aware of and meet these minor needs.

For example, suppose you manufacture and supply shoelaces to boot and shoe-makers. The primary need of the shoemaker is to have a lace that enables their shoes to remain comfortably on the feet of the consumer, without slipping. The shoemaker may also have one or more secondary needs, such as knowing the laces are the right colour, that they will arrive on time and that the price they are being charged is the price agreed. Additionally, the shoe-makers will require the laces to be strong enough to do the job they were intended to do and not break.

Questioning potential buyers closely, and probing for their underlying needs, will also help you overcome any objections that arise during the selling process. Indulging customers by meeting their lesser needs turns satisfied buyers into loyal customers. This objective must be your ultimate aim, because loyal customers put more profits into your business than anyone else.

Improving cash flow

One proven by-product of excellent customer service is the way loyal customers promptly settle their accounts, thus easing your cash flow. Loyal customers do this out of selfish motives because they have no desire to lose the extra service you give them. It is significant to them that their orders arrive on time, and any problems that arise are resolved effortlessly.

Because you know your business-to-business customers more intimately than any retailer can ever know his average walk-in customer, you need never wait for them to complain. Being in a position to telephone a few days after your buyer has received your goods, you can simply enquire about the delivery. Did it arrive on time? Were there any shortages? Has the invoice been calculated correctly? The results of this type of call will:

- highlight any discrepancy and give you time to rectify the problem before payment becomes due;
- get any shortfall or breakages delivered before it becomes a problem for them;
- remove any reason for non-payment when it is due.

Customers will quickly become aware you care about their custom, and will tend to remain loyal to you, not your competition.

Offering the best service in the world will not exempt you from customers who fabricate complaints simply to get extra time to pay. You can only distinguish between genuine and false complaints through perseverance and probing questions. Usually those offering trivial excuses for not paying will try to deflect the conversation away from the main topic. Be professional and always return to the subject matter. Once you return to the main subject, ask for the money they owe you. The customer offering false reasons for non-payment will at this stage come up with a different excuse than the one they originally used. Remain unruffled when speaking to this type of customer and continue to provide them with the same level of courtesy you give all your other customers. Their behaviour will alter in time.

Product development

Did you know that loyal satisfied customers could willingly become unpaid employees of your business? All they need do is promote your business at every opportunity they get. Certainly they will have a greater impact on your profits than disgruntled ones. As you should know by now, customer service is about taking those extra steps to satisfy customers' needs, using positive attitudes.

Listening to what buyers have to say and acting upon the advice they give is good for business. It will also enable you to adapt existing products or services to current marketing trends, and perhaps inspire you to develop completely new lines. Businesses cannot afford to stand still. They must grow. Knowing your customers' needs will help you to evolve.

Products or services can be modified, and new ones created, when complaints are periodically analysed. Customers will tell you if they require an item you do not stock or manufacture. When a large number of customers tell you they are unable to acquire certain items, in-depth research can confirm if a viable market exists and if there is sufficient demand for you to produce it. With the use of a properly construed customer service policy, feedback from customers will continually point the way to new products.

Regularly reviewing those systems you operate which have a direct bearing on your customers' ability to trade with you will do much to improve customer loyalty. When reviewing your system and procedures, you need to be asking questions such as:

Sales order systems	Can the system deal with special orders?
	How easy is it for a customer to place an order?
	When an order is placed, how long is it before a customer receives confirmation?
Delivery systems	Do we deliver when the customer wants it or when it's convenient for us?
	How are customers informed of a delivery time/date?
	Are deliveries always made on time?
Complaints systems	Is it clear whom customers should complain to?
	How fast do we resolve complaints?
	Who analyses complaints and to whom is it reported?
Accounting systems	Are credit terms clearly printed on all invoices, delivery notes, and sales literature?
	How correct are our invoices and is VAT exactly calculated?
	Does the customer know when and where to pay?
Pre- and after-sales systems	Is it easy for customers to contact us?
	Can customer visits be made outside normal working hours?
	How long does a customer have to wait for a spare part?
	What checks are in place to ensure an engineer calls on time?

THE PRIME OBJECTIVE OF ALL SYSTEMS IS TO MAKE TRADING WITH YOU EFFORTLESS.

Customer information

Chapter 6
Customer information

What you'll find in this chapter:

➠ Learning about customers' needs

➠ Making technology work for you

➠ Keeping in touch

➠ Preserving the competitive edge

⚠
CAUTION

PERSONAL INFORMATION STORED ON A COMPUTER IS AFFECTED BY THE DATA PROTECTION ACT 1984. A BUSINESS STORING INFORMATION IN THIS MANNER NEEDS TO REGISTER WITH THE DATA PROTECTION AGENCY, AND BE PREPARED TO UPHOLD THE PRINCIPLES OF THE ACT. CHECK FOR FURTHER DETAILS WITH YOUR LOCAL CHAMBER OF COMMERCE.

The secret to amassing customer information is to ask questions. This can be accomplished by talking to your customers face-to-face, through a telephone call, or by the use of a questionnaire. Once sufficient replies have been solicited, you will begin to build up profiles of your customers.

When you have analysed these profiles, statistics will emerge, providing you with an overall portrait of a typical customer. Additionally, you will obtain precise details about each customer's buying pattern. Furthermore, these profiles will disclose why customers made their purchase from you – or another supplier. Armed with such powerful information, improving products, sales, and developing customer loyalty should prove to be no problem!

Learning about customer needs

An average customer profile will contain a balanced mixture of personal details. Apart from letting you know what their names are and where they live, it will also inform you of any activities they have in common with others who completed your forms. Using this information creatively will help you to lift profits.

In a direct mail campaign, for instance, you could send selective advertising to diverse groups. Let us assume you supply clothing for women. You wouldn't sell much by sending a catalogue of teenage fashions to the over-fifties, would you? Being selective about the names you include in your mail-shot means that sales can be customised and your mailings cost effective. Digital printing makes this possible for even the smallest business.

Most of us at some time in our lives have received a general marketing questionnaire. The market research company will be using the same form to gather information for two or three separate clients. Because of this, the form used will be very general. Your questionnaires, on the other hand, will need to be tailored to your individual business requirements. The form opposite is only a sample, and the questions you could insert are endless.

Based on the information garnered from such a form, a travel agent, for example, would not send cruise brochures if the person responding preferred resort holidays. If this person went on holiday more than twice a year, the agent would probably decide that a mailing sent three or four times a year would be the most effective.

Proper use of these types of form will allow you to spot the higher-value customers, because some customers can be more equal than others in terms of profits. Pinpointing the biggest users from the smallest allows you to rationalise your marketing budget and cut costs. Utilising such customer data to build relationships can transform any business.

Another requirement of your questionnaire, especially if you are in the business-to-business sector, is to distinguish between the buyers and users of your products or services. A buyer in a large firm may be targeted

Customer/Market Research Questionnaire

Title

Telephone no. (day)

Surname

Telephone no. (evening)

Forename(s)

Fax

Address

E-mail

Date of Birth

Postcode

Marital status

Position

No. of employees

Salary range:

£10–15,000 p.a.   £15–25,000 p.a.   £25–50,000 p.a.   Over £51,000 p.a.

Number of children: 0–1   1–2   3–4   More than 4

Do you own/rent: House   Bungalow   Flat/maisonette

How many cars in your family:

1–2   3 or more

How often do you go on holiday each year:

Once or twice   Three or more times

Length of holiday preferred:

1–3 week vacation   Weekend breaks

Type of vacation:

Resort   Cruise

Where did you last buy clothing:

In a departmental store

Local shop

From a catalogue

Do you shop for groceries:

2 or 3 times a week

4 or 5 times a week

Every day

by your salesperson, but it will be the users who will determine whether or not your products are suitable.

Here's a little scenario to demonstrate what I mean: A finance director in a finance house leasing motor vehicles and office equipment will buy the services of a debt collection and repossession company. He will probably never use this service, but his or her employees – credit controllers and manager, collection personnel, and litigation staff – will.

Who do you really need to convince that your products or services are the right ones to choose? In the above situation, anyone other than the finance director would probably be the better target.

The best surveys, irrespective of the method used, not only ask about the product or service ingredients, but also establish the significance each part of your firm has to the customer. Unfortunately, the response rate of questionnaires tends to be low. Offering motivation such as money-off coupons, entry into a prize draw, or perhaps a free sample, can improve the reply rate. However, telling customers how much you appreciate their assistance and explaining the benefits you hope this study will eventually bring them tends to elicit the most satisfactory results.

IN A COMPETITIVE MARKET, IT IS ESSENTIAL FOR SMALL BUSINESSES TO MAXIMISE THE USE OF CUSTOMER INFORMATION TO STAY AFLOAT.

Making technology work for you

Technological advances have made it possible for small businesses to compete equally with their larger rivals. The Internet is fast becoming a popular medium to use when communicating with customers. Gone are the days when the World Wide Web was used solely for sales, including on-line shopping and advertising.

Customer focusing through e-mail makes it cheaper to retain customers longer. In addition to managing customer information, the technologically superior database software can be used to analyse the effectiveness of advertising campaigns, and to customise direct mailing activities. Furthermore, you will find the Internet suitable for:

- purchasing;
- organising travel arrangements;
- recruitment.

The above items are only a few of the innumerable uses to which your computer can be put.

Another advantage technology can give you is through use of the laptop and mobile telephones. Providing sales representatives with these very mobile pieces of equipment allows them to tap into your firm's computer network and obtain up-to-date information about the customer they are calling upon. This is in addition to checking the availability of stock, and suggesting alternatives if required. It can also inform the representative about any outstanding disputes which may affect the customer's judgement when contemplating placing another order with your firm.

Various types of documents can be stored electronically: sales brochures, parts catalogues, plans, and reports. Staff and customers alike can gain access to this material, depending on the restrictions placed on its retrieval. It is not only documents created on a computer that are capable of being stored in this manner, however. With the use of a scanner you are able to convert incoming documents into an electric copy in no time at all.

Many software packages are now readily available. They offer a business a range of options, from simple reporting tools to more sophisticated systems. The simplest software packages to use are those which link staff with all other parts of your business. A more complex package can analyse information as it in inputted, allowing an instant examination of buying trends.

ALTHOUGH THE PRICE OF SOFTWARE IS FALLING, CARE MUST BE TAKEN IN CHOOSING THE RIGHT SYSTEM. THE WRONG PACKAGE COULD PROVE COSTLY.

The most technical of all software is one used for data mining. It enables users to investigate intricate problems not normally encountered. Such a package could reveal how sales of chocolate biscuits would increase if sited on shelves adjacent to tea and coffee displays, but it is doubtful whether it would be suitable for small businesses. The best software packages are those which allow businesses to customise their systems to specific requirements, simply by choosing from a menu of functions. There will always be infinite pressure placed on your time and resources when you're running a small business, but proper use of technology should help you manage your time more effectively.

ALLOW POTENTIAL CUSTOMERS TO E-MAIL THEIR ORDERS THROUGH YOUR WEB SITE, AND EN-COURAGE THEM TO MAKE ENQUIRIES OR COMMENTS AT THE SAME TIME.

Keeping in touch

Information is of little use to you if it's not put to good effect. Today's technology offers opportunities unheard of only a few years ago. Using direct mail, and in particular e-mail, to keep customers informed of new products and services is one thing. Utilising it to obtain feedback, complaints and customers' reactions to the level of service you're offering is another – it is the best business sense. E-mail also acts as an excellent tool to help you keep your customer records updated. The integration of databases provides the added advantage of allowing you to treat customers as individuals. New telephone technology means it is now possible for the address of the incoming telephone caller to be displayed on a screen the instant they get through to your company. Personal details and preferences can also be displayed, allowing dialogue with each customer to be more meaningful. With the integration of customer profiles within your firm, different departments can remain in contact with all customers.

YOU WILL FIND A SURFEIT OF UP-TO-DATE MARKETING INFORMATION ON THE INTERNET. IT'S ALL THERE, JUST WAITING FOR YOU TO LOG ON.

As an example, let's take an average motor dealership. The sales division would need to know the frequency a customer changes their vehicle in order to send a brochure of the latest models currently available. After sending such a brochure, someone in the sales department would then telephone the potential customer to arrange a test drive. At the same time, the service department would need details about the intervals of servicing the customer's existing model, in order to send a reminder. Little touches like these make the customer feel important, and hopefully go some way to retaining his or her loyalty.

The use of databases and mailing lists available on-line is another area of technology that can help you to expand. Lists are available by any criteria you care to use, for example:

- households;
- occupations and leisure interests;

- business type and location;
- number of employees or turnover;
- car or pet ownership;
- name of departmental heads.

There is no combination of yardsticks you cannot request. Once you have made your selection and purchased it, it can be downloaded immediately. You can purchase a list on the Internet either by using a normal credit account, or secured credit card payment facilities. Downloading is either done by a data file suitable for mail-merging, or printed directly onto labels. This latter method is ideal for small businesses as lists can be purchased in small quantities. Sending regular direct mail shots via e-mail is a cheap and effective way of keeping in touch with your customers. With this medium you can also send up-to-date price lists and special offers in small, well-constructed web pages.

Preserving the competitive edge

Personalising customer service through the use of technology will help to preserve your competitive edge. The use of a laptop computer and CD-ROMs makes fashioning impressive presentations to customers' precise requirements fairly easy. Without the time and costs of travelling, long distance demonstrations are also possible via video and data conferencing links. E-mails cut the cost and time of sending quotes, and utilising on-line forms reduces paperwork.

SOME CUSTOMERS WANT THE BEST MONEY CAN BUY, AT THE LOWEST PRICE POSSIBLE. OTHERS REQUIRE QUALITY AND LUXURY, THE PRICE IS IRRELEVANT. TAILOR YOUR CUSTOMER SERVICE TO FIT THE CLOTH.

Retaining the competitive edge in exporting is another advantage of technology. E-mail and web sites are not bound by international boundaries. It takes just as long to e-mail a customer in the next street or town as it does to America or Japan. Video conferencing permits face-to-face meetings with buyers, and an instant demonstration of your products. Rapport with potential overseas customers is quickly established using this media.

Why not publish a list of the most frequently asked questions on your web site, together with the answers, of course? Enabling customers to find solutions for themselves cuts down on the possibility of embarrassing questions arising. Here are a few of the things your

IF A COMPANY POLICY
STIFLES TRADE, CHANGE
THE POLICY OR SCRAP IT
ALTOGETHER.

customers expect from you. If you meet these needs, preserving an advantage will not be too difficult:

- consistency and reliability;
- flexible service;
- confidentiality.

Repeat business is usually the most profitable business; a good after-sales service is essential to keep you competitive. Ensure that all your systems are user-friendly, and that there is no room for misunderstandings of any description. Be sure your customers are informed about the type of warranties on offer, and the parts and service you supply in case of breakdown. These are the sort of things you can do to constantly have an edge over your competitors. Your customers will come running back to you, time after time.

Communicating
with customers

Chapter 7
Communicating with customers

What you'll find in this chapter:

➡ Choosing the right words and stance

➡ Putting yourself in the customers' shoes

➡ Intensive listening

➡ Using the telephone effectively

➡ The written word

➡ A personal view about selecting the right words

AVOID USING JARGON IN ALL FORMS OF COMMUNICATION. CUSTOMERS CAN FIND IT FRUSTRATING IF THEY ARE UNSURE OF YOUR INTENTIONS.

Client information is best gained through active communication with customers. Moreover, at the core of every superior customer care operation rests the art of communication skills. In order to generate a favourable working interdependence with your customers, you must communicate with them in two basic ways:

- by word of mouth – that is, face-to-face in your workplace, at your customers' premises or on the telephone;
- writing – using letters, e-mail, news sheets or memos.

To convey the correct message to our customers, we must use some fundamental rules and a few special skills. In all forms of communication we use words. In a face-to-face situation, we also use body language. On the telephone, the only tool at our disposal, besides our words, is our tone

---

of voice. In our letters, the grammar we use replaces our vocal intonations. To get the correct message across to customers the right balance must be struck.

Choosing the right words and stance

REFLECT ON WHAT YOU ARE ABOUT TO SAY, BECAUSE THE RIGHT WORD IN THE WRONG TONE COULD EASILY IRRITATE YOUR CUSTOMER.

Because some words have different meanings to different people, we ought to choose our words carefully when communicating with anyone outside our immediate family. Take the word 'bread', for example. It could be baked dough, or, as in some circles or areas of the country, it could mean cash. In the south people usually ask for a bread roll; in the north it's a cob. Using abbreviations is another minefield. Unless they are universally recognised, it's best to omit them.

Sometimes we do not do justice to the potential the tone our voices has when we are communicating with customers. Take the word 'sorry', for instance. If spoken softly it can indicate genuine regret. Said in a medium tone of voice, it could be construed as a sarcastic phrase. Uttered harshly and it conveys a 'couldn't care less' attitude. Our voices actually reflect our true feelings, so it is essential to think carefully before opening our mouths. This is especially true when speaking on the telephone.

UNDUE EYE CONTACT, LIKE STARING, CAN MAKE CUSTOMERS FEEL AWKWARD.

We now need to take a look at body language, probably the most powerful mechanism we have to express our feelings. Foremost in this equation is our face, open for all to see and read. Do we come across as smiling and cheerful, or woeful and annoyed? Smiling is the simplest and most effective form of body language we can use, next to eye contact. (However, there are times when smiling can be inappropriate. A smile is hardly the expression you need when facing a customer whose new car has broken down half a mile along the road, just minutes after you saw him off your lot.) Direct eye contact lets the customer know you are really interested in what they are saying. Avert your gaze and the 'I couldn't care less' message comes across.

It is not easy to interpret body language, especially as everyone has their own. In the same manner you convey messages through your body, customers can also pass on to you priceless information about how they are feeling. Generally speaking, anyone sitting or standing erect is usually feeling confident. On the other hand, if someone is feeling nervous or depressed, their shoulders will be hunched and their eyes downcast. When people feel threatened they tend to fold their arms across their body. The next time you are feeling low, try to stand or sit upright and convey a look of confidence, even if you're not. You'll be surprised at what a difference it makes.

note

Sometimes you may have difficulty communicating with certain customers, like those with special needs such as impaired speech, hearing or sight, people whose primary language is not English, or people who are illiterate. In these instances, you will need to demonstrate your most exalted customer service.

Putting yourself in the customer's shoes

Achieving a sympathetic and congenial interrelationship with your customers and colleagues is an essential ingredient for effective communication. Unless you obtain this type of rapport, the customer service you offer will be meaningless. Most of the time this rapport happens naturally, but what exactly is it? Quite simply, it is:

* getting along with people;
* feeling at ease with someone;
* seeing eye-to-eye;
* having empathy with the other party;
* being on the same wavelength;
* feeling comfortable when communicating with customers.

Finding out what customers want and how they feel clearly shows you care and have time for them. At times it will not be easy to get on the same wavelength as your customer, but by being observant and listening carefully to what they are saying, you can overcome this problem. Always put yourself in the customer's shoes and try to match their voice and body language, but do not go over the top. An inappropriate response from you might cause the customer to feel he or she is being mocked.

Intensive listening

When we were at school, a lot of time was spent teaching us to read and write. Unfortunately, no one bothered to instruct us in the art of listening. Whilst hearing is a natural ability, understanding what people are trying to tell us is another matter. We hear, but we rarely understand.

NEVER ASSUME YOU KNOW WHAT THE CUSTOMER IS TRYING TO SAY – IT COULD STOP YOU FROM LISTENING.

FOURTH EXERCISE

1. Listen to a friend read an extract from a book for 3 to 4 minutes.

2. Now write down how much of the passage you can recall.

You will be surprised how little you will remember

Try this test with your colleagues at work, and continue with this exercise until your recollections improve. Listening intently is very demanding, it requires:

- being observant and then displaying your attention by nodding your head or making eye contact;
- reading and digesting body language;
- heeding how things are said, and trying to comprehend the meaning;
- repeating what you have heard to confirm you have understand the message.

Customers will instinctively know when a person is not listening to what they are saying. In fact, they often interpret this sort of behaviour as a form of personal rejection. Shoppers who are made to feel this way will let you know by buying from your competitors.

Most people are easily diverted from active listening. Sudden noises or incidents around you draw your attention away from the conversation, even if only momentarily. When listening to customers is actually part of your job, you will face many of the following obstacles:

- letting your mind wander or becoming bored;
- waiting to get your point across;
- becoming impatient because there's other work to do;
- regretting something you said when you left home in a huff that morning.

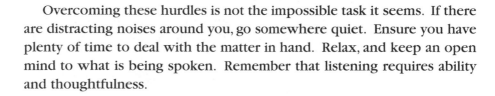

Overcoming these hurdles is not the impossible task it seems. If there are distracting noises around you, go somewhere quiet. Ensure you have plenty of time to deal with the matter in hand. Relax, and keep an open mind to what is being spoken. Remember that listening requires ability and thoughtfulness.

Using the telephone effectively

We use the telephone constantly at work, at home, and with the aid of a mobile, anywhere we care to choose. So what is there to learn? Obviously, when communicating on the telephone, body language is useless to you. The emphasis is now placed not on what you say, but how you say it. As in face-to-face discussions, a smiling face is your greatest asset; likewise a smiling voice on the telephone is equally as important. If you have met the person at the other end, have a mental picture of them throughout the call. When a firm tone is required, stand up. Whether receiving or making the call, always ensure you have a notepad and pen handy at all times to jot down notes.

If you are the one initiating the call, you are automatically given time to prepare. During this time, think carefully about the message you want to get across and the outcome you expect to achieve. If necessary, jot down the main points so they are not overlooked. However, do not attempt to read from a script – it will sound wooden and unnatural. Finally, when you get through to the person you wish to talk to, ask if it is a convenient time for them. If it isn't, arrange a time when you can call them back.

When you are the one to receive a telephone call, stop what you are doing and give it your full attention. Answer the phone with a largish smile and a cheerful good morning or afternoon. Announce yourself by name, and if appropriate, the department you work in, together with the name of your firm. Ask what you can do for them, and listen carefully to what they are saying. Jot down any important points that might arise during the call.

SMILE AS YOU PICK UP THE RECEIVER AND IT REALLY WILL REFLECT IN YOUR VOICE.

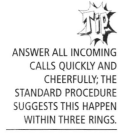

ANSWER ALL INCOMING CALLS QUICKLY AND CHEERFULLY; THE STANDARD PROCEDURE SUGGESTS THIS HAPPEN WITHIN THREE RINGS.

Here are a few other tips you may find useful:

- request the caller's name, and use it throughout the call;
- avoid asking the caller to hold on, or transferring them to someone else;
- if you need to call back, agree a suitable time and call when you said you would;
- as the call ends, go over the main points and confirm the action you agreed;

WHEN RETURNING A CALL, IT IS ADVISABLE TO SUMMARISE THE MAIN POINTS OF YOUR EARLIER CALL.

Before replacing the receiver, always thank them for taking the trouble to call. This relays a vital message to your customer: they and their business really matter to you.

On the other hand, never try to rush a telephone call, as this will convey you cannot be bothered with the person calling. Whether making or receiving calls, remember to speak slowly, clearly and with confidence. Before speaking, it helps to take a deep breath, which clears your head and allows you to concentrate on the matter in hand.

The written word

Productive writing is an essential factor in the maintenance of a caring customer service policy. Try to avoid using angry words, for you will not be able to retract them. Furthermore, any written communiqué must be accurate. The timing of written communications is crucial. Set benchmarks need to be introduced and their compliance strictly observed. These standards could include:

- all letters to be answered with 36 hours;
- quotes and orders must be remitted or confirmed within 24 hours;
- complaints to be acknowledged the same day as they are received;
- customers to be updated in respect of complaints and orders every five days.

One of the advantages of written communication is you have ample time to think about what you want to say. The major disadvantage? Letters are one-sided, providing no opportunity for rapport or an immediate reaction. When composing a letter, there is plenty of time to deliberate upon the message you wish to get across to the customer. Use this time wisely, because as with a face-to-face meeting, your letter must be customer service orientated.

THE MAIN DRAWBACK
OF WRITTEN MESSAGES?
UNLESS YOU USE
RECORDED DELIVERY,
YOU ARE NEVER SURE IF
YOUR LETTER HAS
ARRIVED.

As explained earlier, jargon and abbreviations must be avoided at all costs, to remove the possibility of misunderstandings. Your relationship with the recipient will decide how formal or informal your letter will be, but do not forget that it is a business communication after all. In planning your letter, the following should be considered:

- the purpose of the communication;
- the degree of urgency – when should you write it;
- to whom should it be written;
- what topics must be covered;
- what copy documents are required.

With a modest PC, it is possible for everyone to write presentable letters, memos or eye-catching sales literature. Today's word-processing packages offer spelling and grammar checks, so your letter or pamphlet should therefore be 100 per cent accurate in every way. Any written communication needs to follow a rational order of events that can be understood. Furthermore, it should be:

- clear and to the point;
- courteous and thoughtful;
- interesting, showing the customer they matter to you.

Finally, remember that the first few seconds of any communication lay the foundations for a relationship. In a meeting, it's the first appearance; in a letter, it's the first sentence or two; and on the telephone, it's the first few words you utter. So, make them count.

A personal view about selecting the right words

I do not have the opportunity to fly as often as I would like. Apart from an occasional short-haul internal flight on business, most of my long-distant journeys take place when I'm on holiday. I try to take one trip every year to the United States. I've sampled only a couple of airlines, but the one that stands out in my memory is Virgin Atlantic.

EVERY METHOD OF COMMUNICATION YOU USE SHOULD BE LOOKED UPON AS AN OPENING TO ENHANCE YOUR RELATIONSHIP WITH A CUSTOMER. EVERY FORM OF COMMUNICATION IS AN OPPORTUNITY FOR YOU TO TURN A DISGRUNTLED CUSTOMER INTO A SATISFIED ONE, AND A SATISFIED CUSTOMER INTO A LOYAL PATRON. NEVER MISS AN OPPORTUNITY IF YOU CAN HELP IT.

From the moment I arrive at a check-in desk until the time I disembark at the journey's end, the friendliness of all Virgin's staff is always exceptional. Nothing appears to be too much trouble for them. But what really got me on their side happened on the very first flight I took with them.

No matter what airline you travel with, there is always someone to greet you as you step on board their aircraft. The use of the standard phrase, 'Welcome aboard' is legendary. However, when I stepped on to Virgin's aircraft, I was taken aback by the stewardess's greeting. The words she uttered were unexpected – more personal and friendlier than I had ever heard before.

She said, 'Welcome aboard. I'm so pleased you've chosen to fly with us today.' I always fly economy, not by choice, but circumstance. Adding those few extra words to a standard phrase made me feel like a first-class passenger. To Virgin Atlantic, I was important.

By putting a little thought into the way you approach and greet customers, and the words you choose, you can make the difference between having a one-off purchase, and a whole lifetime of sales.

Getting it right

Chapter 8
Getting it right

Have you ever taken a morning off work because someone promised your furniture would be delivered within a given time frame, only to wait hour after hour before you finally learn that it will arrive 24 hours later than promised? If so, you will know why it is important to get your customer service programme right the first time.

So how do you get it right the first time? We've already spent some time talking about how caring and giving a little extra service will endear your customers to you. Saying 'yes' to the challenge of resolving a customer's problem is also an important factor. All this, in addition to being friendly and enthusiastic, goes along way to getting it right. The incorporation of positive phrases such as the following into your staff's vocabulary will bring undeniable results.

- 'How can I help?'
- 'What can I do for you?'
- 'I'm unable to help but I will get someone who can' (and you do)
- 'The best/fastest/easiest way to solve this problem is!'

'Think customer, think action, and think it now' should be the catch phrase for your business.

Having the best customer care programme around need not cost you any more money than you're spending now. Simply shift part of the resources used on advertising for new clients, and spend it on making existing customers loyal. The return on your investment will be much higher than you can imagine in terms of sales per customer.

Getting it right doesn't mean everything must be perfect from day one. Customer care will have to continuously evolve, and will come about by an ongoing process of development, with everyone in your business striving to provide the best service they can.

To ensure you get it right, here are three things you must have:

- a clear understanding of the aims your business is striving to achieve;
- two-way contact with both external and internal customers;
- an obligation to gather feedback, and relentlessly take action on the information gathered.

Good customer care means continuously improving the service given to your customers, while at the same time balancing the needs of both the customer and your business. But don't forget – the customer must always come out on top!

QUALITY CUSTOMER
SERVICE CAN ONLY BE
DELIVERED THROUGH
ATTENTION TO DETAIL.

Making it happen

Customer service will not just happen, you must make it happen. If you don't, your business will fail. Give customers the best, and they'll expect better, so you cannot afford to drag your feet. Thinking you've gone as far as you can is a defeatist attitude.

Just around the corner, somebody will be hatching new customer benefits, fresh ideals of effectiveness and new courses of action to improve customer loyalty. Being responsive to customer needs signifies your firm has no intention of standing still, that you realise the world is changing and you have no intention of being left behind.

What else is there to make customer service work for you? Here are a few ideas you may wish to use:

CUSTOMER SERVICE POLICIES SHOULD NOT BE CARVED IN STONE, BUT SHOULD BE USED ONLY AS A GUIDE.

- cut out small print on your terms of trade;
- have facilities for children;
- ensure opening and closing times are convenient for the customer, not just you and your staff;
- write instruction manuals that people can understand.

Employees must see you are serious about providing the best customer care possible. If at all possible, avoid using any procedures that make it difficult for employees to provide a first rate level of service.

Nowadays, listening to what customers want and need is not enough. Sometimes you will have to lead customers to what they want before they know it. How many people were asking for Internet services a few years ago? Developing new products without proper research is fraught with danger. Orthodox market research and customer surveys would not have revealed the demand for Internet services a decade ago. Ideas like these only come from inspiration, and a deep insight into the way lifestyles will develop in the future, besides a lot of nerve.

WITHIN YOUR BUSINESS, YOU NEED TO BUILD A TEAM DEDICATED TO PROVIDING CUSTOMERS WITH THE MAXIMUM CARE AND ATTENTION PHYSICALLY ACHIEVABLE.

That's what will make it happen for your business. Once your customer care programme is up and running there is no turning back, it can only go forward. The good thing about this is that it will propel your business forward with it. Some firms have little idea how their customers behold the products and services they provide. Here is one question you must be consistently asking yourself, 'How well am I meeting the needs of my customers?'

Teaching customer service disciplines

Instilling customer service principles can be a waste of time and resources if it is approached in a half-hearted manner. Those at the top must be fully committed to serving the customer and providing 100 per cent back-up. Furthermore, the exercise will be fruitless if customer care skills are not sustained and strengthened afterwards by regular workshops.

Your training programme must include everyone employed in your business. Selecting only those who have continual direct contact with customers should not be a consideration. Customer service must be practised internally if it is to have any chance at all of working or improving. Having customer service regimens working between departments and all employees ensures harmonious relationships internally, and a smooth-running operation, one that will spill over into external customer care. The benefits to a business implementing all-over customer care procedures are immeasurable.

Whenever possible, try to avoid purchasing off-the-shelf video training seminars, because training then becomes too general. A retail business's requirements differ greatly to those trading in a business-to-business environment. Tailor any training directly to your particular business. It will have little meaning to your staff if their actual working surroundings are not accurately reflected in the training they receive. The likely outcome of such poorly-planned training will be employees reverting to your previous, poor standards.

A most proficient method of organising any training agenda is to obtain agreement on its aims, then commit yourself to the changes essential to achieving that end. This will also include deciding upon such things as:

- budgeting for training and incentive schemes;
- performance related appraisals (customer care);
- how the customer service package is to be presented.

At all stages of planning and implementation, all staff members should be consulted. Not only to strengthen your in-house teams, but also because with such involvement staff will be made more aware of your

PRIOR TO PUTTING A TRAINING SCHEDULE TOGETHER, REVIEW EMPLOYEES' ATTITUDES TO CUSTOMER SERVICE BY ASKING THEM TO COMPLETE THE QUESTIONNAIRE IN CHAPTER ONE.

WORKSHOPS WILL NEED TO HAVE A CONSTRUCTIVE APPROACH TO THE TASK IN HAND, CENTERING YOUR STAFF'S ATTENTIONS TOWARDS PROBLEM SOLVING.

customers' needs. Workshops are normally structured around individual departments, like sales or production, but this does not mean customer service will be fragmented. Every section of your business needs to be under a single customer service umbrella, and interactive with each other.

A prerequisite of any training programme is its internal promotion. This enables the ground to be cleared for any fundamental changes that are about to take place. All internal media contact materials will need to be utilised, and the best people to undertake this mission are your marketing team, assuming you have one.

The message any publicity has to get across initially is to inform all employees how they will personally be involved. Next they will need to know what's in it for them, and why improved customer service routines are being evolved. Additionally, the campaign needs to:

- motivate staff;
- encourage change;
- develop comradeship.

Of course, it is a matter of choice, but generally speaking, training is best undertaken in small groups. However, time factors may have a substantial bearing on training numbers in a large business.

In smaller firms this problem does not exist, and training everyone at the same time generates a sense of belonging. Employees can now see themselves as part of the whole business. The same effect can be obtained by including a departmental cross-section in each workshop for large organisations. Smaller groups also allow for more individual input and performance feedback.

Video training can help overcome two of the more pressing problems you might encounter when training the entire work force – finding the time and the location. However, there are drawbacks to this method inasmuch instant feedback and personal input are non-existent. However, if you bring in desktop video data conferencing, staff will not even have to leave their desks. Interactive training courses of this nature are ideal, especially if you have branches dotted around the country.

STAFF WILL BE BETTER ABLE TO ABSORB THEIR TRAINING IF THEY RECEIVE IT IN SHORT SPELLS, AS OPPOSED TO A ONE- OR TWO-DAY INTENSIVE COURSE.

WHEN PUTTING TOGETHER A CUSTOMER SERVICE TRAINING SCHEDULE, REMEMBER ROLE-PLAYING IS A FUNDAMENTAL REQUIREMENT TO ENSURE ITS SUCCESS.

CUSTOMER SERVICE NEEDS TO BE CONTINUALLY REPACKAGED AND TRAINING CONSTANTLY REINFORCED. OTHERWISE, YOUR STAFF WILL FORGET THE BENEFITS IT CAN BRING.

Using this method of training offers another major advantage; by recording and storing the training material on your computer network, staff can train at their own or the company's convenience.

For significant improvement to take place, start your customer service training from the top, never the other way round, from the bottom upwards. Management training for both senior and middle management should provide a perception of the commercial usefulness positive customer service will bring to the firm. If this is carried out properly, an endorsement and commitment for a lasting customer loyalty programme should be the end result. Support of middle management is crucial to guarantee a successful outcome, since resistance to change manifests itself most often through this section of any company.

The precise content of any training session will vary from firm to firm, but almost everyone can gain from mastering communication skills such as listening, questioning, and interpretation and study of body language. Other areas, like problem solving, or using the telephone, may only be applicable to a few businesses.

PRAISE STAFF WHO TAKE THE INITIATIVE AND MAKE CUSTOMER CARE THEIR FIRST PRIORITY.

All managers must actively participate in developing the customer care programme, not sit back and hope someone else will get on with it. This is essential if the training is to be effective. Only management can produce the techniques for making customer loyalty happen from the top and continue all the way down the line. Therefore, management has a duty to provide their employees with:

- a rationale for why the firm is instigating action on customer service;
- methods of improving performance;
- practical workshops to boost relevant skills performance;
- commitment to the proposed changes.

Both senior and middle managers must be prepared to devote more of their time to customers and their needs. Only by meeting and talking with clientele will management learn if their new customer service initiatives are working.

Motivating employees

One of the two major constituents of motivation is self-esteem, the other is reward, although reward on its own does have a couple of shortcomings, as we shall see a little later. First of all, let's take a look at how egos can be a forceful cause of action.

Self-esteem is at the heart of a person's individuality. Cast aspersions on their actions and they will be humiliated. Employees who have their self-respect assaulted will have little incentive to provide the standards of customer service you require and customers deserve. On the other hand, boost their self-esteem and an employee's performance will be enriched. This in turn will manifest itself in positive actions, thus enhancing the level of service. Encouragement drives employees to take an extra step, thereby helping turn satisfied customers into loyal ones.

JOB SATISFACTION, IN ADDITION TO RESPECT FROM THEIR PEERS AND EMPLOYERS, IS SOMETIMES ALL THE MOTIVATION CUSTOMER SERVICE PEOPLE REQUIRE.

Reward is usually taken to mean monetary gain, or promotion. Whilst there is a little self- interest in all of us, on its own, a reward of this nature generally offers very little long-term advantage. Staff who provide customers with first rate service purely for cash can be classified as selfish. Customers will be quick to see through their masquerade and whilst they may remain satisfied, loyalty will not be upper most in their minds.

Let's be honest, all of us tend to do things in the name of self-interest. Human nature being what it is, if we can maximise the benefits for ourselves, we do. Acting in this manner is not selfish. However, when behaving in this fashion, most of us are inclined to take into account the impact our actions will have on others. Monetary awards should not be offered every time a member of staff smiles at, or speaks civilly to a customer. Rather, it should be restricted to suggestions made by staff for improving overall service to customers. This way, employees are not only permitted, but positively encouraged to have a personal input into your business. Employees who can see their ideas working, or who are know that if they, too, put forward suggestions they will be explored, will have commitment. It is this commitment which is the best form of motivation you can get.

People with a commitment to their employer will act favourably towards customers because they find serving them innately fulfilling. This positive attitude will be reflected in their words and in their body language. Customers will not feel intimidated, so a sense of loyalty will begin to develop.

It is far better to keep personal stimulants within a regular appraisal system than to offer more direct inducements. Such a system, coupled with the commitment idea earlier mentioned, will help to reinforce your customer service beliefs. As well as generating an improved working atmosphere, these methods will also drive customer service forward.

AWARDING INDIVIDUAL PERFORMANCE CAN BE DANGEROUS, BECAUSE IT ENCOURAGES IN-HOUSE COMPETITION AT A TIME WHEN YOU SHOULD ALL BE WORKING TOGETHER.

Accrediting employees to settle local disputes on the spot can be cost-effective. Customers who receive instant gratification over an initial grievance will be more likely to accept smaller compensation than if they have to wait for a supervisor or manager to become involved. Rewarding better customer service is probably the hardest award system to put into practice. A commission based on increasing sales and bonuses for productivity is easy to measure. Instead of looking at ways to set and measure individual customer service targets, perhaps a profit sharing incentive is a better way forward. Wasn't your customer service initiative begun to improve customer satisfaction, then implemented to turn all your satisfied customers into loyal customers and increase profits?

The original business motive behind your customer service drive was to generate sales, to ensure better cash flow and to increase profits. Therefore, profit sharing will enhance team bonding and drive your customer loyalty programmes. If you do insist on recompensing individuals for outstanding achievements in customer service, here are a few tips you might find helpful. Reward for:

- actual productivity, instead of stock takes;
- endeavours directly related to upgrading customer service;
- behaviour which sets good standards for others.

Awards of this nature need not cost the earth. In one of the finance houses I worked, gift vouchers were awarded each month for the best all-round performance. The winner received £20 and was asked to select a department store of their choice in which to spend this sum. The runner-up received £15, and the person who placed third, £10. In a transport business, the prize for the women was flowers and a bottle of wine for the men, . Cash is never your only option. Always make the award presentations in public, and remember to thank the winners for their efforts. On the other hand, don't neglect to recognise the achievements of the rest of the work force.

Measuring performance

IF YOU REALLY WANT TO KNOW WHAT PEOPLE THINK OF YOUR BUSINESS AND SERVICE, ASK A DEPARTING EMPLOYEE – THEY'LL PROVIDE THE MOST INTERESTING INFORMATION!

We discussed previously how difficult it is to measure customer service performance. Quantifying courteous service to the extent customers will want to return and buy from you again, or repeatedly use your services, is indeed difficult. The introduction of a customer complaints system will help you to measure the improvements in resolving customer problems more accurately.

Customers' reactions to your levels of service and how you meet their expectations can be judged by using customer feedback, and utilising the methods which have been mentioned throughout this book. For example:

- customer surveys and questionnaires;
- talking to customer at the time of the sale;
- telephoning them after the event;
- observing customer reactions and listening to their conversations.

Another method is to be your own customer. Better still, get a friend or member of the family to do this for you, someone unknown to your employees. This ploy is usually referred to as 'mystery shopping'; there are even organisations who you can pay to do it for you.

If you're a retail business, get your 'shopper' to call at your shop two or three times, with at least one of these visits made just before closing time. The shopper should be instructed to ask a member of staff a direct question such as, 'Do you have these shoes in a size 12?' and then check to see if the staff member keeps looking at their watch, especially if this visit is made near closing time. The shopper should also make note of whether or not the staff member pays attention to what they have just said. An average mystery shopper will:

- note the time they entered and left the store;
- state the day and date of their visit;
- see how long it is before a member of staff approaches;
- make a note of the approximate numbers of staff and customers in the store;
- comment on the salesperson who assisted them, for example, did they
  - smile and make eye contact?
  - smile without eye contact?
  - not smile, but made eye contact?
  - offer neither a smile nor eye contact?
- were they satisfied with the service received?

A simple YES/NO response to all of these questions will be sufficient.

For those trading in a business-to-business situation, go out of your office and telephone your own business with a complaint. Make a note of how the telephone was answered. Was the member of staff both cheerful and helpful? Call prior to, or at opening times, and just before closing time as well, for the same reasons as mentioned above. Additionally, make sure that you call after hours, to check out your voice mail message. Is it friendly?

When running the training workshops suggested previously, make sure that your employees are given the opportunity to bring to light all the good things that have happened to them. At the same time, give them a chance to let off steam, without repercussions, and moan about all the bad things that went wrong. No matter where or how you gather your information, chances are it will still be valuable. Don't simply file it away but take action. Do something positive and do it now.

What's next?

All that remains now is to ensure you maintain the high levels of customer care you have started. The secret is to keep the ball rolling. Don't let up on excellent service, because if you do, your competitors will not. To keep the ball rolling, your business will have to maintain a relentless level of improvement. Ensuring that this happens requires:

- knowing what you wish to accomplish;
- meeting performance benchmarks;
- seizing the day, and taking continual actions to improve the level of customer care you offer.

Providing good customer service means that you take responsibility for never missing a chance to put your customer first. In order to achieve this goal, every contact or communication must be sales orientated to show the customer you care. Customers are the reason you are in business, don't let them or yourself down.

Before finally putting this book down it's time to retake the personal attitude test set in the first chapter. Hopefully, your new score will have improved considerably!

Index

More MADE EASY™ books...

Look out for the Professor! Made Easy Guides are practical, self-help business reference books which take you step by step through the subject in question.

- ■ Legal and business titles
- ■ Experts' advice
- ■ 'How to' information and instructions
- ■ Save professional fees!

Company Minutes & Resolutions

Company Minutes & Resolutions Made Easy is what every busy company secretary or record-keeper needs. Maintaining good, up-to-date records is not only sensible business practice, but also a legal requirement of Companies House. This Made Easy Guide makes the whole process straightforward. It provides an invaluable source of essential documents that no company should be without.

Code B501 • ISBN 1 902646 41 X • 250 x 199mm
paperback • 190pp • £9.99 • 1st Edition

Debt Collection

Chasing debts is pain which all businesses can do without. Unfortunately, unpaid bills are an all-too frequent problem for business owners and managers. *Debt Collection Made Easy* helps you solve it. It provides expert advice and tips on resolving disputes, reducing the risks of bad debt, getting money out of reluctant payers, letter cycles, credit insurance, export credit, and much more.

Code B512 • ISBN 1 902646 42 8 • 250 x 199mm
paperback • 134pp • £9.99 • 1st Edition

Employment Law

Written by an employment law solicitor, *Employment Law Made Easy* is a comprehensive, reader-friendly source of reference which will provide answers to practically all your employment law questions. Essential knowledge for employers and employees!

Code B502 • ISBN 1 902646 40 1 • 250 x 199mm
paperback • 142pp • £9.99 • 1st Edition

... to order, simply call 020 7940 7000 or visit www.lawpack.co.uk